DATE			

SIEGE

Castles at War

SIEGE
CASTLES
AT WAR

Written by Mark P. Donnelly & Daniel Diehl

Illustrations by Robert Rich • Photographs by Dick Clark

Taylor Publishing Company
Dallas, Texas

Page ii: Caerphilly Castle in Wales provides the background for the action shots in this book.
Page vi: Bodiam Castle was built during the closing of the fourteenth century with profits from the Hundred Years' War.

Designed by David Timmons

Published by Taylor Publishing Company
1550 West Mockingbird Lane
Dallas, Texas 75235
www.taylorpub.com

Library of Congress Cataloging-in-Publication Data
Donnelly, Mark P.
    Siege: castles at war / by Mark P. Donnelly & Daniel Diehl ;
photographs by Dick Clark ; illustrations by Robert Rich.
        p.   cm.
    Includes bibliographical references and index.
    ISBN 0-87833-213-8
    1. Siege warfare—History. 2. Sieges—Europe—History.
3. Castles—Europe—History. I. Diehl, Daniel. II. Title
UG444.D66   1998
355.4'4—dc21   98-37703
                                                        CIP

Printed in the United States of America
10 9 8 7 6 5 4 3 2 1

"The fact is that everyone has his own idea,... usually corrupt, of the middle ages.... Only we monks of the period know the truth,.... but saying it can sometimes lead to the stake."
—Umberto Eco, *The Postscript to the Name of the Rose*

This book is dedicated to the memory of Jean de Froissart and all of the other medieval chroniclers whose works are excerpted in this book. His eyewitness accounts shed a light of immediacy onto distant and faded historical events, and to them we owe much of our understanding of the medieval world.

CONTENTS

acknowledgments

The production of this book required the assistance of a great many people, and we gratefully acknowledge their help. Because this is a companion work to the documentary film *Siege: Castles at War*, we are especially grateful to EMS Productions, Hilversum, Netherlands, for granting us literary rights to the story. Mounting a medieval siege of the scale shown on these pages would not have been possible without the backing of a television production company. We are especially grateful for the assistance of Leo van der Goot, Mark Verkerk, and Adair Osbaldeston for their continuing help and support. Tremendous thanks are also due to Cadw (Welsh Heritage) for putting up with us during eleven days of mercurial November weather.

Thanks, too, to our on-site photographer, Dick Clark, and all the other individuals, groups, and organizations who allowed us access to their photographic libraries, including the City of York Council, Haddon Hall in Derbyshire, David Lazenby, and the Middelaldercentret medieval history center in Denmark.

A very special thanks to Bob Rich, our graphic artist, who produced the wonderful medieval maps, drawings of siege engines, and numerous spot illustrations that appear throughout this book.

We are also grateful to all of the people who took part in the reenactment of the siege itself, including, but certainly not limited to, Keith Piggott, Ben Piggott, Chris and Val Sage, Henry Clayton, Alan Gibbon, Mark Danbury, John White, Gary Waidson, the staff and friends of Cosmeston Medieval Village in Cosmeston, Wales, Paul Denny and Artefacts, Legio Secunda Augusta, and the dozens of reenactors who worked very hard through some very long days. Without all of their help, good cheer, and enthusiasm, *Siege: Castles at War* would simply not exist.

PREFACE

This book required the combined efforts of many people from several countries. Originally developed by the authors as a television documentary commissioned by Discovery Network, USA, we have used our script as a starting point for this greatly expanded work. Because of the time constraints inherent in television programing, we were convinced that a subject with the massive scope of medieval siege warfare could only be adequately addressed in written form. Consequently, with the kind permission of European Media Support, producers of the documentary, we have undertaken this book to expand and elaborate on the information presented in the documentary.

It seems only fair to explain our approach to the project. This book uses live-action photographs taken during the filming of the documentary, combined with a fictionalized siege, to depict medieval warfare, rather than relying on manuscript illuminations and photographs of ruined castles, which is the most accepted approach in similar historical works directed at the popular market. The primary limitation of literature dealing with medieval warfare, even in those books which are scrupulous in their approach to history, is a lack of immediacy. No matter how commendable the scholarship of a modern author, the fact of the matter is that none of us has ever engaged in, nor witnessed, an actual medieval battle. We can only rely on accounts of the period to guide us.

To compound the problem of immediacy, the only historical, visual representations of medieval life are manuscript illuminations drawn by chroniclers and scribes of the period. While they provide important historical reference material, the cartoonish renderings do not communicate to modern readers—who are accustomed to the most graphic representations of their world—any sense that these are depictions of real, and often horrific, events. Manuscript illuminations simply do not impart the scope and horror of the hand-to-hand combat that was central to medieval warfare; neither can they explain the sophisticated technology needed to construct the massive military machinery that made effective siege warfare possible. It is our hope that by including graphic representations of a reconstructed medieval battle, this book will take on the immediacy of a television news program, the means by which most of us now experience political and social conflicts taking place throughout our world.

To provide the text with the same intimacy and immediacy as the photographs, we have included actual accounts of numerous sieges and battles written by a variety of medieval chroniclers and historians, many of whom were witness to, or involved in, the battles which they describe. Unfortunately, because chronicles were often commissioned by or for members of the nobility, they routinely ignore the role of the common soldier. We hope that by augmenting these accounts with information taken from historical records, military account books, and other historical sources that accu-

rately convey the composition of medieval armies, this book helps to put the common soldier, and his role in the medieval siege, into historical perspective.

By and large castles, and the lives of those who lived in and fought over them, are central to our concept of the Middle Ages. Unfortunately, our understanding of how the castle actually functioned, both in peace and in war, has been distorted by popular literature and Hollywood. The central figures in the "pop-culture" version of medieval history are the brave knight and a just, if stern, king (who looks in all likelihood like Sean Connery). In the popular romantic view of the Age of Chivalry, a column of knights (unfailingly in highly polished, matching armor) rides across the drawbridge of the castle to meet the enemy in glorious hand-to-hand combat. In the day's battle to save honor and truth, many may die; but few will die slowly from blood loss after writhing in pain for hours or even days. So much for Hollywood.

What is missing in this popular mythology of the Middle Ages—other than common sense—is any evidence of the common man. Peasants and yeomen made up the great bulk of medieval society and the medieval military. As with fighting men throughout history, the majority of soldiers who engaged in medieval battle were commoners. When a conflict resulted in a siege, as many of them did, those taking part in the fighting were frequently peasant conscripts, hired mercenaries, and commoners employed as archers and engineers. Some were hurriedly assembled peasant levies thrown into battle with virtually no training, while others were highly trained professionals. Whatever their status, they shared one common bond: They were despised by the chivalry whom they served. To a great extent, this book is their story.

We could have relied purely on the

chronicles and historical records, supported by archaeological and historiographical information, to construct a general overview of siege warfare, but instead, we decided to enhance our firsthand approach by creating a fictitious siege, which serves as a framework around which we weave the historical information. There was probably no such thing as a "typical" siege. Each siege was entirely different. The mentality and temperament of the belligerent commanders, the materials and skills available at the moment, and the size and geographic location of the castle or town being besieged all contributed to the specific tactics employed. The chances of the great range of siege tactics described in this book being employed at any one siege is extremely unlikely. But by creating a fictitious siege, supported by historical evidence, we can bring the entire breadth of the medieval arsenal into play.

Through this multifaceted approach to medieval military conflict, we hope to answer the most basic and most often misunderstood questions about siege warfare. What comprised a siege? Who was involved in them? Why on earth would anyone besiege a castle when it is so much easier to simply bypass it? Why was the mounted, armored knight considered the indomitable force on the medieval battlefield, and what were the causes of his decline? Why don't people build castles anymore? What changed that caused the siege to go out of fashion? To answer these and other common questions about warfare during the Middle Ages in clear, concise text, and with vivid pictures, is our goal in *Siege: Castles at War*.

The first two chapters of this book contain very brief looks at the origins and development of castles and siege machines. While neither of these is integral to describing a medieval siege, they are nonetheless important if we are to understand why the medieval siege developed as it did, and frankly, even we found the ancient origins of castle-like fortifications and sophisticated siege tactics outlined in these chapters startling in their sophistication. Chapter 3 addresses the historical framework in which our imaginary narrative takes place. It outlines the major events of the Hundred Years' War (the pinnacle of castle effectiveness) and serves as a brief look both at major field engagements and at the often complicated political (and personal) factors that lead to such brutal conflict. In similar fashion, the last two chapters deal with gunpowder and the final disappearance of the castle. These, like the opening chapters, are not necessarily integral to medieval siege warfare, but again we felt that the information helped complete the reader's understanding of why, and how, the medieval siege finally came to an end.

We hope that the information in these chapters, combined with the accounts of medieval siege warfare in the intervening chapters, will provide our reader with a better and more balanced understanding of the motivations behind medieval conflict and the makeup of the armies who fought in them. In the final analysis, warfare in the Age of Chivalry, like warfare at any time in history, was not the least bit glorious. It was bloody, brutal, terrifying, and horribly cruel. Those who lived through it hired chroniclers and storytellers to make their deeds sound glorious to lessen the horror and pain of what they had lived through. Once we come to grips with this fact, we can begin to understand the Middle Ages as something other than a world of chivalric fantasy born in the romantic writings of Sir Walter Scott and in the production studios of Hollywood.

Chapter One

IN THE BEGINNING

Ancient Siege Warfare

He shall set engines of war against
thy walls and with his axes he shall
break down thy towers...
—Ezekiel 26:9

For as long as humans have been building cities, they have felt the need to defend them against attack—and to destroy the fortifications built by their enemies. Virtually every known civilization learned to construct some type of fortification to protect their homes and property. Ancient fortifications took two distinct forms; either they encompassed entire towns, creating walled cities, or they were strictly military outposts.

In prehistoric northern Europe, where man had not yet perfected the art of slaughtering his neighbor with organized tactics and complex machines, most settlements depended on simple earth ramparts surrounded by deep ditches to defend inhabitants. When these Iron Age settlements came under attack, the defenders left the safety of the packed-earth forts and fought in the fields beyond. We can assume this was an effort to keep invaders as far from their homes and families as possible. On the other hand, in the more sophisticated Middle East, technology had already begun changing the face of warfare.

The most straightforward way to protect personal property has always been to build a high fence around it. To the ancients, it must have seemed logical that the simplest way to protect a settlement was to build a wall around it as well. Walled cities showing surprising levels of sophistication, in both design and execution, existed in the earliest recorded civilizations and are still in evidence at such places as Jericho, Troy, Babylon, Asshur (Assyria), Thebes (Egypt), Mycenae (Greece), Rhodes (Greece), Alexandria (Egypt), and Tarragona (Spain).

For a few short centuries, heavy walls provided adequate deterrence to virtually any form of direct attack, serving as ample protection against foot soldiers armed only with spears and knives. It would be several centuries before any practical means of breaching the walls would be devised—Joshua and his army of Israelite trumpeters not withstanding.

Before the invention of siege weapons, and even later in instances where siege engines were impractical or unavailable, a direct siege could only succeed by mounting an escalade. In the escalade, crude ladders were set against fortress walls, and wave after wave of attackers, armed with sword and spear, were sent up the ladders to face the wrath of defenders stationed on the walls.

While defensive walls protected cities from being overrun, they also inadvertently spawned the starvation siege. When there was no way to get through or over a wall, one effective alternative was to blockade the city gates and wait for the inhabitants to surrender. Starvation sieges, however, were time consuming and left the besieging forces vulnerable to attack by disease or a relieving force. Few ancient armies were willing, or tactically sophisticated enough, to use a blockade effectively. Still, the developing importance of siege warfare in the ancient world must not be overlooked. If we are going to understand the siege's place in medieval society, we must examine its origins and the degree of importance it was afforded by classical generals. If we look at the exploits of Alexander the Great, Hannibal, and Julius Caesar, we can see that prominence as a military leader in the ancient world depended on becoming a master of the siege.

The Biblical World

Not surprisingly, some of the earliest literary references to siege warfare, and occasionally even to siege engines, can be found in the Old Testament. In the second book of Chronicles, we find the story of the Israelite King Uzziah, who was obviously a force to be reckoned with: "[Uzziah] went forth and warred against the Philistine, and brake down the wall of Gath, and the wall of Jabneh, and the wall of Ashdod..." (II Chron. 26:6). And later we read of an impressively sophisticated approach to engineering for the time: "Moreover [Uzziah] built towers in Jerusalem at the corner gate, and at the turnings of the wall, and fortified them" (II Chron. 26:9). There is even a reference to what appears to be a bolt-firing ballista: "and [Uzziah] made in Jerusalem engines, invented by cunning men, to be on the towers and upon the bulwarks to shoot arrows and great stones withall..." (II

Chron. 26:15). In the book of Ezekiel we find: "And they shall destroy the walls of Tyrus and break down her towers" (Ezek. 26:4). Unfortunately such references, though tantalizing glimpses into early defenses and siege warfare, give us almost no specific information as to the actual nature of the weapons, the precise construction of the defenses, nor, unfortunately, can we depend on the accuracy of the accounts. To find more reliable data on the nature of ancient warfare, we must turn to archeological excavations and early graphic representations of weapons and fortifications.

At ten thousand years old, Jericho may be the oldest city in the world. It is certainly the oldest known city for which massive fortification walls have survived. Archeological evidence tells us that by 7000 B.C.E. the town was surrounded by a defensive wall 10 feet high and 13 feet thick. The thickness of the walls indicates that they were used as defensive positions from which soldiers could hurl spears and rocks at would-be attackers. There are even surviving remnants of at least one stone tower; located at a bend in the wall, the tower contained a spiral staircase, also of stone, built directly into the structure of the tower. It is an amazing comment on the course of civilization and human priorities that technology sophisticated enough to build such impressive defenses developed more than three thousand years before the invention of the bow and arrow.

By 3500 B.C.E.—the approximate date of the first known use of the potter's wheel—Babylon, capitol of the Babylonian empire, was surrounded by a steep-sided moat and a wall twenty-three feet thick and strengthened by towers built at regular intervals along its perimeter. Due to the eventual destruction of the city, the original height of walls and towers is unknown. Sometime around 2700 B.C.E., Babylon's neighbor, the city-state of Uruk, then under the leadership of the legendary

Gilgamesh, was fortified by a great wall, supposedly punctuated with 900 towers.[1] It seems that these cities may have needed such elaborate defenses. By 3000 B.C.E., Babylon's major competition for political dominance in the region, Sumeria, may have developed tactics specifically for use in the siege. Understandably, the Sumerian capitol at Ur was as heavily walled and fortified as any of its neighbors.

The Hittites, who rose to prominence around 2000 B.C.E., used multiple lines of defensive walls around their cities and an additional fortified wall protecting the royal palace in the center of the town. As early as 1200 B.C.E., the Hittite city of Dapour was surrounded by a double line of curtain walls, the inner most of which contained a rectangular keep. Because this was about the time that Moses is said to have led the Israelites out of bondage, it may give us a picture of the sophistication of Egyptian fortifications of the same period. Arguably, the Hittites were the first to use this "concentric ring" form of fortification, which reappeared as the pinnacle of the medieval castle development. However, this type of fortification would not evolve in Europe until 1300 A.D., fifteen centuries after its appearance in the ancient world.

Egyptian tomb paintings show that the Hittites also constructed "hoardings," wooden fighting platforms, on their city walls to give wall guards a clear shot at approaching enemy soldiers—another development usually associated with the castles of medieval Europe. The Egyptians pioneered the use of the architectural buttress to support the weight of massive fortification walls surrounding the cities along their southern border, an innovation which they may have adopted from the architecturally precocious Hittites. But the protection offered by these impressive fortifications would not go unchallenged for long.

By the mid twelfth century B.C.E.,

Assyrian King Nebuchadnezzar I had begun to flex his political and military muscle by instituting a campaign to establish himself as the only recognized god in greater Mesopotamia. An army supposedly numbering 170,000 infantry and 12,000 cavalry was sent out under General Holofernes to impose the new religion throughout the area and destroy the temple in Jerusalem. Directly in their path lay the Israelite walled city of Bethusia. Ever innovative, Holofernes instituted one of history's earliest recorded starvation sieges in the hope of taking the city without sacrificing any of his own men. In a little over a month, the city's water supply began to run dry and Bethusia was on the verge of surrender.

Without doubt, the city would have capitulated had it not been for the wiles of Judith, a beautiful widow from Bethusia who insinuated herself into Holofernes' camp under the ruse of having escaped the city to offer her assistance to the great general. Over dinner that night, Judith managed to get the Assyrian general so drunk that he passed out, allowing Judith to kill him, cut off his head, and escape back to Bethusia, completely demoralizing the Assyrian troops in the process.

The loss of Holofernes not withstanding, the Assyrians continued their aggressive military policies and between 800 and 700 B.C.E. were directly challenging the Hittites through an extended campaign of sieges against their cities. Unlike the Hittites, the Assyrians had learned how to effectively breach fortification walls. Sometime between 800 and 700 B.C.E., the Assyrians rose to power, sweeping away the Hittite empire by breaching the walls of their fortified cities.

This drawing, taken from a stone relief carved around 750 B.C.E., shows troops under the command of Assyrian General Tiglathpileser besieging a fortress. Note the scalers using ladders to reach the top of the fortified walls, a tactic strikingly similar to that which would have been used throughout the Middle Ages.

Carrying out aggressive campaigns against worthy enemies and helpless victims alike, the Assyrians protected their own citizens by employing the well-established precaution of walling their cities, while simultaneously devising weapons that assured their armies victory over any city they singled out for punishment. Indeed, the warlike Assyrians were probably the originators of the siege engine. They developed both the battering ram and the siege tower, giving them the option of entering an enemy city by going over or through its walls. The first military tactician known to specialize

ANCIENT GREECE

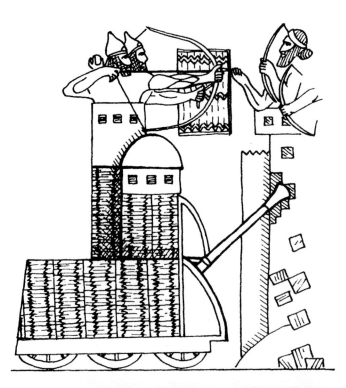

A siege tower that might have been the enemy of many medieval fortifications is employed by Assyrians in the ninth century B.C.E. In addition to towers of multiple heights, the base of the tower sports a battering ram that seems to be making short work of the fortified city walls. Note that the entire structure is set on wheels and seems to be protected with mats of woven rushes.

in the art of siege warfare was the Assyrian King Tiglathpileser III, who ruled from 746 to 727 B.C.E. Under his reign, not only were the siege tower and battering ram put to constant use, but history's first full-time corps of engineers was also established to ensure that both weapons and tactics be constantly improved. The new technology proved stunningly effective. Shortly after 700 B.C.E., Assyria breached the walls of Babylon and destroyed the city, and in less than a century, they had captured Memphis and Thebes in Egypt, and forced Judea to pay tribute.

During the thirteenth and fourteenth centuries B.C.E., the Greek city-states built elaborate defensive walls around their cities and palaces, which would have looked familiar to any student of medieval architecture. The city of Mycenae even had an entry gate defended by twin towers and several sets of siege doors.

The longest running military action to take place between these fortified Greek cities were the Trojan and Peloponnesian Wars, the most infamous engagement undoubtedly being the siege of Troy itself. The story of the Trojan War has been kept alive for us by the poet Homer, who recorded the events of the war, three and a half centuries after the fact, in his epic poems *The Iliad* and *The Odyssey*. Today, such stories featuring gods and superheroes are certainly considered works of fantasy, but they are not without at least some basis in fact.

Historically, the Trojan War was a ten-year struggle carried out between 1203 and 1193 B.C.E. by the federated cities of Greece against the Trojan city-state. The war culminated in a three-year standoff at the heavily fortified city of Troy. The ruse of the infamous Trojan horse was a final, desperate attempt by the Greeks to gain access to Troy. According to legend, an immense wooden horse was constructed, supposedly as an offering to the goddess Minerva. The Greek army then boarded their ships and apparently set sail for home. The Trojans, seeing the Greeks in retreat, rushed out to take possession of the horse and hauled it into their city. As night fell, dozens of Greek soldiers who had hidden themselves inside the hollow statue crept out under cover of darkness and opened the city gates for their comrades, who had returned during the night. In proper heroic tradition, the Trojans were slaughtered for their "crimes."

In all likelihood, the fall of Troy probably had more to do with military horsesense than with wooden horses. What the story tells us is that all attempts to breach, or overwhelm, the defenses of Troy were in vain. But, as we shall see, things that cannot be accomplished with brute force can often be achieved through more subtle methods.

As time went on, such tactics became an increasingly important factor in determining the outcome of major engagements. Around 400 B.C.E., the city-state of Syracuse (Sicily) introduced the catapult and ballista[2] into the world's arsenal of siege equipment; and while the new weapons may have been used haphazardly, it would not be long before both were exploited to their full advantage. By the second century B.C.E., the military engineer Phylos of Byzantium devoted the majority of his career to developing practical, functional siege equipment as well as tactics for their use. Among his works were improvements on the catapult and ballista and theories on how best to employ them. Thoughtfully, he recorded his work in a nine-volume treatise, much of which still survives. But Phylos was a scientist and engineer. To fully appreciate and apply all the developments in siege technology required a military leader with courage and vision. The first man to successfully embrace the concept of siege warfare as a primary weapon, rather than a tactic of last resort, was almost certainly Philip of Macedon.

Ruling Macedonia, Greece, from 359 to 336 B.C.E., Philip used the siege like a scalpel, carving an empire he could confidently pass on to his heirs. When Philip besieged the fortress city of Echinus, he built two immense siege towers, each three stories in height and equipped with a battering ram in the base. There were fighting platforms at various levels inside the towers and another one on the roof designed to hold a ballista. Inside the towers were cauldrons of water for putting out fires started by the enemy's flaming arrows. The siege towers were rolled into position in front of two close-set towers on the city walls. In the area between the siege towers, Philip's engineers built a rampart of earth, topped with a wooden stockade fence, to conceal the activity of miners tunneling beneath the city walls. Behind the siege line, Philip placed a battery of three catapults to hammer at the wall day and night. After a few weeks of this relentless pounding, Echinus surrendered.

The lessons of Philip's successes were not lost on his son, Alexander. Thanks to a far better understanding of siege technology than any general in the lands he conquered, Alexander would build the largest empire the world had seen to date and come to be known as Alexander the Great.

CLASSICAL GREECE

One of the first inventors (as opposed to military engineers) to devote his efforts to the construction of siege engines was Archimedes, the Greek mathematician. His designs for the defense of Syracuse, in its struggle against the Romans in 212 B.C.E., provided a heroic, if ultimately futile, defense. Among Archimedes's numerous weaponry designs were cranes and massive catapults, both intended for use in naval engagements. The catapults were designed to fire ship-to-ship as well as pound shore defenses. One such catapult, mounted on the deck of the Greek vessel *Syracusa*, could reputedly, if improbably, hurl a stone ball weighing more than 170 pounds a distance of 200 yards. Huge balance-arm cranes were equipped with grappling hooks, on the end of a cable, designed to catch and overturn enemy ships, though how they could accomplish such a feat is unclear.

The infamous Spartan city-state was probably the first western power to make the art of war a full-time occupation, but the reputation of the Spartans as an aggressive and warlike people makes this hardly surprising. What is surprising is that even philosophically oriented Athens surrounded itself with a series of stout siege walls. The innermost set of walls surrounded the temple compound on the Acropolis while another larger wall enclosed the city at the base of Acropolis hill.

Attempts to undermine city walls probably began soon after the construction of the first fortification walls, but written accounts of mining operations survive from no earlier than the time of ancient Greece. The most detailed account of a mining operation during the Greek classical period was written by Herodotus. According to Herodotus, at the siege of Barca (Libya) in 510 B.C.E., the defenders attempted to detect the presence of Persian miners by placing brass shields on the ground near the base of the city walls. Some of the shields rested directly against the walls to pick up and magnify any vibrations caused by the miners digging; others were laid flat on the ground near the foot of the walls and filled with water in the hope that any underground activity would agitate the surface of the water. These crude seismic detectors seem to have worked. Where mining was discovered, the Barcaeans dug countermines into the Persian tunnels and killed the attackers, saving their city from destruction. The disadvantage of this method of mine detection is that mining can only be detected once the miners are already beneath the walls. During this early period when mines were primarily used as a passageway into the fortification, the defenders could countermine and attack the invaders. In later centuries, when the primary purpose of the mine was to

collapse a section of wall or a tower, by the time any vibration was detected, it would be too late to take counter measures.

The Roman Empire

The Romans, who contributed so much to the art of war, also contributed to the art of siege. Rome's major contribution to siege warfare lay in making siege engines smaller and lighter. Where earlier engines were massive brutes that had to be wrestled from one position to another, Roman engineers developed weapons that were lightweight and easily transported. Roman ammunition seems to have been as innovative as their weapons. By burying a small stone ball inside a much larger ball of baked clay, Roman engineers produced a highly effective fragmentation grenade, which, on impact, would fill the air with hundreds of razor-sharp pottery shards. Not a particularly effective weapon in attacking a fortified wall, but ideally suited for use as an antipersonnel weapon. This was the primary intent of the small, lightweight ballista and catapult the Roman army took on campaigns into the unknown territories beyond the ever-extending borders of the empire.

The Romans introduced their vast and improved arsenal of siege weapons into the heart of western Europe during a phase of colonial expansionism that took place in the half century just prior to the birth of Jesus. During campaigns into Gaul and Germany, each legion of 6,500 men was accompanied by an artillery corps of thirty engines of various sorts, as well as the engineers necessary to man them. This was the time of General Gaius Julius later know as Julius Caesar, who was

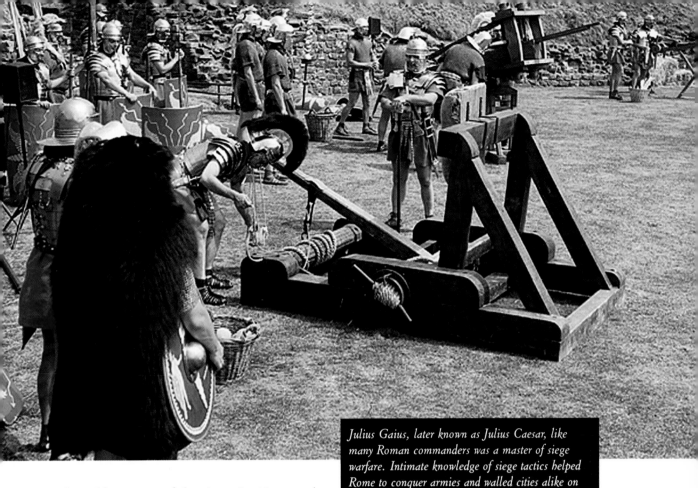

himself a master of the siege. In 52 B.C.E. he laid siege to the fortified city of Alesia in Gaul. By innovative tactics and prudent deployment of men and machines, he brought down the garrison and drove back a relieving army of 250,000 Gauls with a force of only 70,000 legionnaires.

Roman engineers were not deterred, however, if siege engines were unavailable or the terrain was unsuitable for their use. In numerous instances, the Romans simply built earth ramps to the top of an enemy's walls and sent their legions pouring over the enemy battlements. This low-tech but ultimately effective tactic allowed the Romans to overwhelm and defeat the Israelite defenders at the fortress of Masada in 70 A.D.

Rome's rapid growth as a military power made it an obvious target for any other up-and-coming empire of the day. To protect the capital city, the Romans began encircling Rome with a massive fortification wall as early as 578 B.C.E., a project which took forty-five years to

complete. When the Roman republic evolved into imperial Rome under the Caesars, the city's defensive measures were expanded to fit its new marshal image. The wall that eventually encompassed the city was twelve miles long, twelve feet thick, and nearly sixty feet high. There were projecting towers every 100 feet, and each tower was fitted with arrow loops and topped with crenellated battlements[3]. These same innovations would not appear as standard features in northern European fortifications for nearly a thousand years.

Even in its most far-flung provinces, Rome undertook the construction of monumental fortifications. In Britain there were fortified encampments and towns surrounded by stone walls, at such administrative centers as Colchester and London, and at points where an enemy might launch an invasion, such as

Left: The Romans probably inherited the technology for this stone-throwing 'ballista' from earlier civilizations, but made full use of its potential. With innovative missiles and streamlining techniques this became one of the most versatile engines in the Roman arsenal.

Right: An easily portable, lightweight version of the ballista, called a 'catapulta' by the Romans, was developed as a bolt-throwing antipersonnel weapon. At two hundred yards, it could plow through two or three men with ease, or nail a fully armored man to a tree. Photos courtesy of Legio Secunda Augusta

Portchester and Pevensey on the south coast and Hadrian's Wall on the Scottish border. Hadrian's Wall was a monumental attempt at defensive fortification. Built between 117 and 138 A.D. at the order of Emperor Hadrian, the fifteen foot high, seven foot thick wall stretched from the channel coast to the Irish Sea, a distance of over eighty miles. At four-mile intervals along the wall stood fortified garrisons, and between the garrisons were watchtowers. Even in the German provinces, the Romans built a great stone wall running from Coblenz on the Rhine to Eining on the Danube, a line considerably more than the eighty-mile length of Hadrian's Wall. Other similar fortress walls were built in such far-flung provinces of the empire as Syria and Bulgaria.

At about this same time, a fortified tower-palace built at Axum, Ethiopia, may have been history's first castle with a central keep. Whether Rome influenced its construction is arguable; certainly connections between the Romans and the nearby Egyptians existed. Any cross-cultural influences at work in this case probably came from the eastern territories of the Roman Empire, rather than from Rome itself. The eastern empire was rapidly developing into an independent (and heavily fortified) civilization.

The protection of borders was essential to preserving the integrity of the Roman Empire; and the more important the province, the more impregnable its fortifications. The eastern arm of the Roman Empire, known as Byzantium, was important enough that it warranted the very best defenses that could be devised. By the second century B.C.E., the Byzantine Romans built walls around their cities engineered to withstand catapult and ballista shot weighing up to 350 pounds—not that such a weapon was, or physically could be, constructed, but the mere threat of their existence prompted the Byzantines to undertake extraordinary measures to protect themselves. Stories of such monster weapons seemed real enough that Byzantine mathematicians calculated the weight, trajectory, and distance that such machines might be able to throw a ball and dug

steep-banked dry moats 500 yards beyond the outer perimeter of their city walls to keep their nightmares at a safe distance.

Even as Rome began to collapse under the combined weight of a corrupt bureaucracy and an overextended empire, it continued to expand and develop defenses. The administrative center of the empire was shifted from Rome to Constantinople, the capital of Byzantium. From Constantinople, a new empire, separate from Rome, began, reclaiming and expanding the eastern-most frontiers of the old empire. To effect this expansion, the Byzantines had to cope with changing times and the new, more mobile fighting tactics employed by the Arab tribesmen who surrounded them. By the sixth century A.D., Byzantine general Belisarius constructed fortified compounds in North Africa with a

Left: This wall of shields, known as the 'tetsudo' or 'iron turtle,' allowed Roman legions to walk into hails of enemy arrows and spears with relative safety. A similar formation was used during the Middle Ages to allow ramming parties, miners, and others to approach the walls of a castle.

Right: The catapult, known to the Romans as an 'onager,' is probably one of the oldest siege engines on earth. An onager of this size would have weighed nearly a half ton and would have launched a ten- to twelve-pound rock up to five hundred yards. Photos courtesy of Legio Secunda Augusta

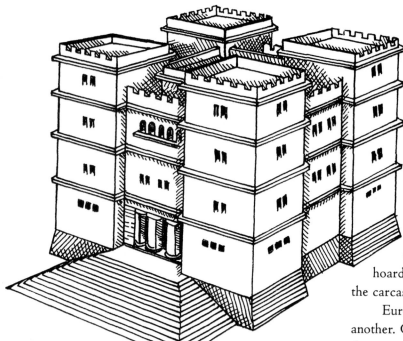

large defensible tower in one corner, intended for use as a last refuge should the fort be overrun—a notable precursor of stone castles with a tower keep.

While the Byzantine Empire protected itself from its enemies through an aggressive program of fortification and military development, the remnants of the Roman Empire in the west were faring less well. Into the vacuum created by the collapse of Rome, barbarian hoards descended like vultures to pick at the carcass of the once-great empire.

Europe reeled from one onslaught after another. Civilization was reduced to little more than warring tribes slaughtering each other with abandon in search of power and plunder. The Dark Ages had descended on Europe, and the accumulated knowledge of the classical world was in danger of being lost. The only answer to the chaos gripping Europe would be the reintroduction of effective fortifications on a broad enough scale to ensure social stability.

the rock and the hard place

Castle Evolution in Medieval Europe

Just as changes in climate promote evolution in nature, political conflict fosters social change and invention. Centuries of hostilities between the medieval kingdoms of Europe brought about the most architecturally and militarily advanced castles in history while simultaneously inspiring the means for their destruction. By the beginning of the fourteenth century, both the castle and the art of siege warfare were approaching their pinnacle of effectiveness. To grasp the concept and nature of medieval siege warfare, we must understand the general chronology of castle development.

As we discovered in the previous chapter, massive fortifications were not unique to the Middle Ages. From Iron Age hill forts to fortifications enclosing entire cities, the world is littered with monumental defenses that stretch into the mists of time and legend. All of these ancient fortifications took one of two forms: Either they encompassed entire towns or they were strictly military outposts. In the early medieval period, however, the opposing concepts of private residence and military installation merged into the new architectural form which we now recognize as the castle.

THE BIRTH OF EUROPEAN CASTLES

When the Roman Empire dissolved during the fifth century, it left behind a vast network of towns and fortifications. Wherever possible, local cultures reused the abandoned Roman buildings in an attempt to preserve some semblance of civilization. From the southern tip of Sicily to Hadrian's Wall in Britain, Roman fortifications, roads, and civilian complexes became the centers of the few stable communities surviving in Dark Age Europe.

This turbulent world was made up of small, isolated societies adrift in a vast and unforgiving landscape. Miles of trackless forests and open plains were protected only by tiny armies operating under the patronage of minor princes and dukes who were only theoretically responsible to anyone for their actions. These petty noblemen and their cohorts lived where they chose and took refuge where they could.

The wandering barbarian tribes that plagued Europe between the sixth and tenth centuries never developed a system of permanent fortifications. Consequently, both military and domestic construction during this period was carried out with whatever materials and technology were at hand. When new towns and forts were built, it was far more likely that they would be built with wood than stone. Wood was familiar, adaptable to shifting population centers, and in abundance nearly everywhere. The availability of wood eliminated the need to transport stone from quarry to construction site, over miles of rough terrain.

Some degree of political stability was brought to Europe in the late eighth century when Charles, King of the Frankish Empire, codified the knightly orders of chivalry and introduced the feudal system of land tenure. In effect, Charles declared that, henceforth, the richest and most powerful warriors in his kingdom would be granted custody of vast tracts of land in exchange for swearing an oath to defend the Holy Church and their king. In a time when the only tangible form of power and riches came from land ownership, the offer was hard to refuse. This new system of military rulership was eagerly embraced throughout western Europe and earned Charles the sobriquet "Charles the Great," or as we know him, Charlemagne. With the codification of laws came the widespread adoption of socially acceptable goals and norms. With consistent standards of military behavior came a model for constructing fortifications throughout the fledgling empire. Feudalism, the knight, and the castle were born.

Early European castle builders had ample opportunity to see the progress their counterparts outside Europe had made in the art of fortification; they even had occasion to test the strength of their neighbor's walls. Charlemagne's expeditions into Moorish occupied Spain, probably led by Roland, involved at least one prolonged siege and certainly taught Charlemagne the value of stout fortifications.[4] At Sarragosa, Charlemagne's army surrounded the walled city and besieged it over a period of months, but the walls and gates easily withstood all attacks and the invaders were forced to withdraw. Fortunately the lessons learned in Spain did not go to waste.

In 861, Viking armies made a massed attack into the heartland of Europe. In response to the onslaught, Charles the Bald—grandson of Charlemagne—commanded that the construction of military bases take precedence over all other activity. In the year 885, a flotilla of Viking ships sailed up the Seine and into the heart of Paris but was routed by a barrage from over a hundred catapults[5] that had been mounted on the city's defensive walls specifically for the occasion.

The siege of Paris aside, the threat of widespread Viking incursions demanded that a large number of outposts be built throughout western Europe in a relatively short period of time. Consistency and standardization of design were crucial if the plan was to succeed.

Because of the chaotic state of early medieval politics, these forts were never intended to be more than bases from which knights could launch punitive raids against their neighbors and to which they could safely return. Although these first castles were more public shelter than private stronghold, they provided safety from attack and helped extend military supply lines, allowing knights to capture and hold more territory than ever before.

Motte and Bailey Castles

The basic pattern adopted for these fortifications consisted of little more than mounds of earth and wooden stockade fences. Collectively referred to as the "motte and bailey" design, this is the earliest recognized style of castle.

The motte was simply a steep hill of packed earth supporting a watchtower adjoining a yard (or bailey) surrounded by a timber stockade in which men and animals could seek refuge. Mottes varied in breadth and height, but they were at least large enough to hold a lookout tower and frequently a small command post. Over 70 percent of mottes were no more than 20 feet high though some, like Clifford's Tower in York, England, exceeded forty feet. The soil to build the motte came from excavating a defensive trench around the base of the motte and the adjacent bailey yard. The larger the bailey area, the longer the trench needed to surround it, producing more dirt to build a larger motte. Around the perimeter of the bailey, immediately inside the ditch, the construction of a ten- to twenty-foot high timber wall, or palisade, would keep out unwanted visitors.

These early castles were not only defensively and architecturally crude, but their position in the social and political landscape was severely limited. While noblemen owned or controlled the motte and bailey castles, they probably never considered them a home. Castles of this period were often only a residence of last resort, to be occupied during all-too-frequent periods of open hostility.

Over the next century and a half, the castle's role grew and evolved to assume a more central place in the social life of the developing kingdoms and their emerging noble class. By the turn of the millennium, much of the turmoil of the Dark Ages was waning and the castle had assumed its place as the most dominant feature on the political and physical landscape of Europe. The chronicler Lambert d'Ardres wrote about a wonderful timber castle built not far from Calais in the eleventh century. He describes an elaborate structure of many stories and multiple rooms, suggesting that some early castles must have been virtual wooden palaces. These would have been the exception. Most timber castles were more function than form.

Although they were quickly built, and militarily adequate for their time and place, motte and bailey castles had certain undeniable limitations. No matter how strongly defended or how well built a timber castle was, if an enemy could drag a pile of brush to the foot of the stockade wall and set it on fire, even the strongest timber castle could be brought down.

As political boundaries in western Europe stabilized, so did the castles used to defend them. Unfortunately, the establishment of stable borders meant that there were no more barbarian lands to raid in the name of king and church.

Here we see the castle in its earliest medieval form, the motte and bailey. The dirt removed during the excavation of the dry ditch was piled into a hill (or motte) on the central island—the bailey yard. A stockade wall was then set up along the inside of the ditch, and a look-out tower was built on top of the motte. Crude and unimpressive by later standards, the motte and bailey nevertheless provided a place of safety and a means of keeping watch on the surrounding countryside.

This illustration, adapted from a scene in the Bayeux tapestry, shows how easily the wooden fortifications of even the most well-built motte and bailey castle can be reduced by fire. Although they were far quicker to build than stone castles, wooden forts had obvious limitations. Note the soldier on the right surrendering the keys to the fortress under the threat of fire.

Jean de Colmieu, writing about 1130, described a more typical motte and bailey castle in the same region:

It is the custom of the nobles of the Neighborhood to make a mound of earth as high as they can and dig a ditch about it as wide and deep as possible. The space on the top of the mound is enclosed by a palisade of very strong hewn logs, strengthened at intervals by as many towers as their means can provide. Inside the enclosure is a citadel, or keep, which commands the whole circuit of the defenses. The entrance to the fortress is by means of a bridge, which rising from the outer side of the moat and supported on posts as it ascends, reaches the top of the mound.

The extent of the warring between noblemen, and the degree to which these battles were played out by using a castle as a retreat from which raids were launched specifically to terrorize the peasantry of a neighboring nobleman, is evident in this quote from William of Malmsbury's *Chronicle of the Kings of England*, written around 1140:

There were many castles throughout England, each defending their neighborhood, but, more properly speaking, laying it waste. The garrisons drove off from the fields both sheep and cattle, nor did they abstain either from church yards nor churches. Seizing such of the free peasantry as were reputed to be possessed of money, they compelled them by extreme torture to promise whatever they thought fit. Plundering the houses of wretched husbandmen [farmers], even to their very beds, they cast them into prison; nor did they liberate them, but on their giving everything they possessed or could by any means scrape together, for their release. Indeed, at the insistence of the Earl of Glouchester, the legate, [and] the bishops, repeatedly excommunicated all violators of church yards and plunderers of churches, and those who laid violent hands on men in holy and monastic orders…but this attention profited but little.

The lack of unclaimed territory, however, did nothing to lessen the acquisitive nature of Europe's petit nobility, and they began to fight among themselves for control of estates, dukedoms, and kingdoms throughout Europe.

Castle building took on a new dimension as the nobility went into a construction frenzy, defending themselves and their land holdings from the covetous gaze of their neighbors. The positioning and construction of castles was no longer an accident of fortune; it became a science. Geographical considerations such as the natural defensive qualities of cliff edges, rocky escarpments, rivers, roads, or best of all, a combination of several of these elements could add greatly to the effectiveness of a castle. Shortly after the Norman conquest, Geraldus Cambrensis (Gerald of Wales, 1147–1223) described a castle in Pembrokeshire as follows:

Manorbier [castle] … is excellently well defined by turrets and bulwarks, and is situated on the summit of a hill, extending on one side toward the seaport, having on the [other]… a fine pond under its walls, as conspicuous for its grand appearance as for the [impassible] depth of its waters, and a beautiful orchard on the same side, enclosed on one part by a vineyard, and on the other by a wood, remarkable for the protection of its rocks, and the height of its hazel trees. On the right hand of the promontory, between the castle and the church, near the side of a very large lake and mill, a rivulet of never-failing water flows through the valley, rendered sandy by the violence of the winds. Towards the west, the Severn Sea, bending its course to Ireland, enters a hollow bay at some distance from the castle, and the southern rocks, if extended a little further to the north, would render it a most excellent harbor for shipping.

DEVELOPMENT OF THE STONE CASTLE

The first attempts at creating castles entirely out of stone may have taken place as early as the middle of the tenth century. But it was not until the First Crusade (1096–1099), when European noblemen and military engineers encountered the Byzantine and Moslem fortifications mentioned in the first chapter, that the engineering

A medieval manuscript illumination shows masons constructing a stone wall.

principles of building with stone—and the distinct advantages—became clear. Technologically challenged Europeans must have been awestruck at their first sight of the Byzantine capital of Constantinople. The entire city was encircled by a double row of stone walls, the inner wall being over fifteen feet thick and fifty feet high, with mural towers every sixty yards. The outer wall was only half the height of the inner one, but it was protected by a moat surrounding its entire two-and-a-half-mile perimeter. Armed with a vast store of knowledge and visions of impregnable fortifications, the Europeans returned home and began to create a new and improved generation of castles.

The layout of the first stone-built castles retained the familiar motte and bailey ground plan, with several significant alterations. The first step toward the fully developed castle in Britain was the creation of the "shell keep." In this arrangement, the motte was retained and the bailey yard was reconstructed in masonry. A circular stone wall, known as a "curtain wall," replaced the palisade, and the buildings in the bailey yard were built around a central courtyard with their walls serving as buttresses to support the weight of the curtain wall. The motte, with its watchtower, remained the primary observation point for the castle.

Around the same period, the first major change in castle design took place when the scattered living quarters in the bailey yard were combined into a single rectangular tower called a keep or donjon. With no windows on the ground floor and the main entrance a full story above ground level, these "tower keeps" were far more compact and defensible than shell keeps. The walls of the keep were pierced with arrow loops facing every area of the bailey yard, so the keep could be defended even if the inner ward of the castle had been overrun by enemy troops. Because of its

height, the roof of the keep provided an additional line of defense and a point from which the surrounding countryside could be monitored. This eliminated the need for constructing a motte.

Most early keeps were quite small, measuring only 35 to 42 feet. In these early keeps, the rooms were no larger than the combined thickness of the walls. Thus, a 35-foot wide keep had a living space of only 17.5 feet surrounded by walls 8.75 feet thick. But the tower keep soon grew to truly impressive proportions. The world's most famous keep, the Tower of London, is 90 feet high, and the great keep at Rochester Castle (Rochester, England) soars to 113 feet.[6]

When a keep was built, the motte tended to be eliminated for two reasons. Stone construction allowed structures to be built tall enough to provide adequate lookout points without the aid of a towered motte. In addition, the weight of a stone keep was frequently more than a manmade hill could withstand. Occasionally, through successive rebuilding of an existing castle, a new stone keep was located on top of an old earthen motte. No matter how many innovations were introduced, some castles tenaciously retained elements of wood-and-earth defenses, and a few timber castles remained in use until the Renaissance.

When castles began to be converted from wood to stone, more towers were added to the curtain walls both for defense and to enhance structural integrity. By 1200, virtually all castles had enough mural towers to defend the entire circumference of the curtain wall, and for the first time, towers appeared on either side of the main gate. Soon the towers were fitted with arrow slits to provide safe firing positions from a variety of heights. The appearance of these multiple towers tells us that the castle's defensive emphasis was shifting from the keep to the curtain walls. The outer walls had become the primary line of defense and the keep—with its all important domestic quarters—had become a refuge of last resort.

Early mural towers were either square or rectangular, and while they may have provided

Chepstow is an ideal example of an early castle that evolved and grew over an extended period of time. The first recorded fortress on this rocky escarpment overlooking the Severn River between England and Wales was a motte and bailey castle built between 1069 and 1070. Fifty years later the great tower keep, one of the two oldest surviving in England, was erected.

Over the next three and a half centuries, Chepstow was expanded and improved at regular intervals. One after another, bailey yards and outworks were absorbed into a complex maze of walls, gates, and mural towers. As an important outpost on the Anglo-Welsh border and home of such powerful men as William Marshall, Chepstow was embellished with every technological improvement short of tearing down the existing structures and building an entirely new castle.

This tower is pierced with arrow loops designed to accommodate both longbow and crossbow. The vertical arrow loops, although only three inches wide on the outer face of the wall, widen on the inner face to allow the archer to move from side to side. This allows the archers to cover a wide field, while remaining well protected from attacks directed at them from the outside. The horizontal opening allows a crossbowman a similar freedom of movement. Note that the base of this tower has been thickened with an extra layer of stone designed to withstand the shock of a battering ram.

The crenellations in this wall have been fitted with shutters which can be opened and closed with the aid of an iron prop. When open, the shutter helps protect a soldier from arrows falling from above, and when closed, allows him time to reload his bow in safety.

a clear view of the stretches of wall separating them, there were blind spots around the base of the towers where an enemy could hide. By 1220 towers, like the keeps before them, were being converted from square to round. Round towers offered both an improved line of vision and greater strength, the cylindrical shape being less vulnerable to mining.

At about this same time, areas of wall between the towers were embellished with crenellated battlements, alternating open spaces (through which arrows and other mis-siles could be flung) and small sections of wall (behind which archers and soldiers could hide). The open spaces, or crenels, were sometimes fitted with hinged shutters that could be closed for additional protection when soldiers reloaded their weapons or escaped momentarily from the confusion of battle.

Early in the twelfth century, the inability of guards to fire at an enemy standing directly beneath them at the base of the wall was eliminated by the development of hoardings, wooden sheds cantilevered beyond the walls of the castle. The outer wall and roof of the hoardings provided protection for those inside, while arrow loops in the wall and trapdoors in the floor allowed a clear shot at any would-be attacker. By the fifteenth century, hoardings were frequently replaced by machicolations, a

Left: Wooden hoardings extend beyond the walls of a castle to give the defenders a clear shot at attackers below and in front of the walls while remaining relatively impervious to attack.

Below: An improvement on wooden hoardings, machicolations provided wall guards with the ability to aim their weapon at an enemy near the base of the castle walls without leaning over the edge of the battlements and exposing themselves to enemy fire.

widening of the parapets allowing the battlements to project slightly beyond the face of the wall, much like a balcony. The floors of these machicolations were fitted with holes through which death could be rained down on those below.

THE ULTIMATE CASTLES

The art of making war underwent massive changes during the two centuries following the Norman Conquest of England. The arsenal of siege weapons inherited from the Romans was augmented by new weapons such as the trebuchet,[7] capable of delivering a massive payload, and by new mining techniques that could collapse even the strongest castle wall.

To counter this increasingly dangerous array of weapons, castle designers decided that stout fortifications were no longer enough. The roofs of keeps and towers were altered, enlarged, and strengthened to hold projectile-throwing engines similar to those in the arsenal of the besieging army. The keep and curtain wall were further protected by a complex series of entrenchments, or concentric rings, which allowed defending forces to fall back in stages toward the inner ward should an enemy prove too strong in its assault on the castle. To increase the efficiency of these rings of

A variety of the defensive measures included in the fully developed concentric-ring castle can be seen here. At the far left, a bridge (once a drawbridge), crosses a moat situated between the outer and middle walls of the compound. Sections of the crenellated outer wall can be seen at the center of the foreground. At the top of the picture lies the third and innermost ward, with the keep towering at its center.

defense, the height of the fortification walls increased as they neared the keep. Having lower walls set in front of higher ones allowed defending forces to concentrate several ranks of fire on an enemy force. The distance between the multiple sets of walls was kept uncomfortably narrow to prevent enemy forces that managed to breach the outer defenses from having enough space to muster a sufficient force to assault the inner walls.

The theory behind concentric-ring fortification is simple: The more complex the maze of defenses separating the outside world from the keep, the more time and opportunity the defenders have to resist an invading enemy, or to be relieved by outside forces. To a large extent, the theory worked. Thanks to complex and impenetrable defenses, a small band could hold a castle against a sizable attacking force. In 1294 only thirty-seven English soldiers defended Harlech castle against an entire Welsh army.

In a fully developed concentric-ring fortification, the outermost defensive obstacles were rings of earthworks sometimes stretching more than a hundred meters (325 feet) beyond a castle's curtain walls. These outworks included a wet moat, one or more dry moats, and in some instances, mazes of earth ramparts, which served as breastworks to protect defending troops and make any direct line of approach by an enemy nearly impossible. In

The barbican gate was the forward-most protective structure of the castle. Usually set beyond the moat, or ditch, the barbican guarded the bridge which led from the outside world to the main gate of the castle.

Beyond the barbican lay the main gate-house. Heavily fortified and bristling with guards and protective devices, the gate house was designed to ensure that the largest opening in the curtain wall did not become a weak link in the chain of defenses surrounding the fortress.

Murder holes and sluice ports, such as this one over the main entrance to a gate house, allow guards to rain arrows, boiling water, pitch, and quick lime on the heads of an enemy foolish enough to assault the main gate of a well-defended castle.

The gate house at Caerphilly shows the variety of obstacles constructed to keep out unwanted visitors, including a drawbridge, siege doors, and portcullis.

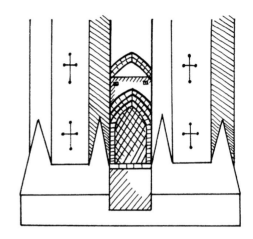

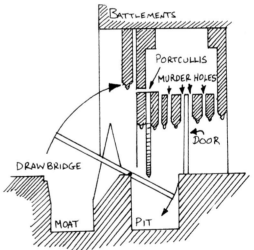

particular, these obstacles prevented moving heavy siege equipment within firing range of the castle walls. No matter how complex the maze of ditches and banks, usually only the innermost ditch, the one most likely to be filled with water, required a bridge to cross.

Behind the earthwork defenses were the vastly more complicated masonry defenses that comprised the castle complex. With the approach to the castle better protected than ever before, it was important that the point of entry also receive special attention. Beyond the formidable obstacle of the drawbridge, the entry gate was protected by a series of heavy wooden siege doors which could be secured with draw bars. Behind the doors were portcullises, heavy wooden lattice works sheathed in iron which could be raised and lowered from inside the gate house to block access to the entry passage. In the walls of the

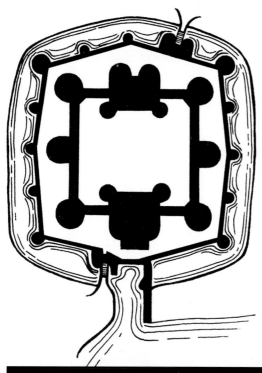

This drawing of Beaumaris castle's concentric-ring defenses shows how the 'rings' worked to protect the lord and the garrison. An outer set of walls controls access to the moat, the outer ward (the area of land between the outer and middle set of walls), and an inner barbican gate that guards the draw bridge crossing the moat. The island is protected by a second set of walls, slightly higher than the outer walls. This wall is protected by the main gate and wooden hoardings, which can be seen on top of the walls to the left and right of the main gate. Beyond the main gate is the middle ward, and at its center lies the inner ward, including the keep at the heart of the castle. Here, in the keep (or donjon) behind walls up to twenty feet thick, is the residence of the lord and his family, the audience hall, and public rooms. It is here, should the rest of the castle be overrun by an enemy, that the garrison would take refuge.

passageway were arrow loops and in its ceiling were "murder holes" through which arrows, boiling liquids, and quicklime could be dropped on unwelcome visitors.

By the end of the thirteenth century, the gate house had grown in importance and mass

until it was the largest and most heavily fortified section of the castle. At Caernarvon Castle[8] in Wales, the "King's Gate" was fitted with two drawbridges, six portcullises, and five sets of doors, along with arrow loops, murder holes, and a sharp, right-angle turn in the middle of the passage. Considering such formidable defenses, anyone foolish enough to stand before the entry gate of a major castle, with any but the most benign intentions, made themselves vulnerable to assault from almost every conceivable angle.

With the development of the concentric-ring defensive system, the keep was moved out of the center of the bailey yard and integrated into the newly enlarged and fortified gate house. Henry III's Montgomery Castle (1224–35) was the first British castle to incorporate many of the defensive aspects of the keep into the gate house. The main gate of Montgomery occupied the entire south face of the curtain wall. By combining the massive protective walls of the keep with the bristling fortifications that had been added to the gate house, the structure was nearly impregnable.

Under England's Edward I (reigning from 1272–1307), the concentric-ring castle reached its most evolved and formidable state. For a combination of complex defensive measures and sheer bulk, it would be difficult to top Edward's fortresses. Between 1277 and 1289, the king kept over four thousand workers busy constructing eight new castles in Wales and added the latest innovations and improvements to over a dozen others. At Conway Castle, one of Edward I's finest concentric-ring castles, access to the royal apartments could be gained only by going up a steep stairway, over a drawbridge, and through three heavily defended gateways each of which was exposed to wall guards on every side.

To the medieval mind, the castle was the most intimidating force on earth next to the wrath of God, and with good reason. Castles were purpose-built to command and defend, protect and subdue. As time passed and castles became more and more capable of defending themselves and their neighboring communities, the social system of which they were a part became more and more stable. But what happens when an army arrogantly ignores the hard-learned lessons of castle tactics and blunders, time and again, into the open field to face an enemy with superior battlefield techniques?

A fully developed, concentric-ring fortification such as Caerphilly Castle in Wales (shown here) provided an imposing, and virtually impregnable, symbol of royal power.

One of the earliest Edwardian castles, and quite possibly the most fully developed of the style, is Caerphilly Castle in Wales. Begun in 1267 by Gilbert de Clare, Earl of Glouster, Caerphilly is still one of the most intimidating structures imaginable. Enclosing over thirty-five acres within its massive curtain walls, Caerphilly is one of the largest castles in Great Britain, exceeded in size only by Windsor and Dover Castles, both of which are still holdings of the Royal Family. This architectural monolith was built on three islands in the center of a thirty-acre lake. On the central and largest of the islands stands the castle itself. The fortress has a double set of concentric-ring walls and four massive gate houses, the outermost reachable only by crossing two drawbridges, and another incorporating a keep. There is also a free-standing tower keep in the middle of the compound.

This engineering marvel was completed in less than twenty years, with most of the work being built in the four years, from 1268 to 1271. This magnificent ruin serves as the background for the action photos in this book and the EMS/ Discovery Network production *Siege: Castles at War.*

Chapter Three

NOBLE ADVENTURES

The Hundred Years' War

> *I have always made inquiries to the best of my ability about the exact course of the war, and other activities... between the English and the French.... In order that the honourable enterprises, noble adventures and deeds of arms which took place during the wars waged by France and England should be fittingly related and preserved for posterity, so that brave men should be inspired thereby to follow such examples, I wish to place on record these matters of great renown...*
> —Jean de Froissart, *Chronicles*

To understand the nature and tactics of siege warfare, it is important to understand the social and political environment that promoted violent conflict during the Middle Ages. It is also important to look at the consequences of engagements in the open field that encouraged commanders to seek refuge behind castle walls. Our concern here is with the events of the Hundred Years' War which was both the climax and turning point of the castle's effectiveness. If castles were so effective, why did knights leave them to engage an enemy in the open field? What sort of tactics were used in field engagements and which mattered more: overall numbers or the composition of an army?

ORIGINS OF THE WAR BETWEEN ENGLAND AND FRANCE

The origins of the war itself are complicated, as such matters tend to be. Let it suffice to say that through inheritance and intermarriage, the English Crown held vast amounts of land and powerful titles in France, as well as claims to the Duchy of Normandy, which had been tied to the English monarchy since the Norman Conquest in 1066. The English claim to these lands, and by extension to the French throne itself, served as catalyst for the Hundred Years' War. The kings of France could never accept that the English held a large part of the Aquitaine in southwest France. The kings of England, for their part, had never forgotten or forgiven their loss of Normandy to France during the unhappy reign of King John in the early thirteenth century.

To complicate matters further, Edward III of England (reigning from 1327–77) claimed the French throne by right of his mother Isabella, daughter of the French King Philip IV. However, the "Sallic Law" in effect at the time invalidated any claims derived through matrilineal descent. The French, therefore, flatly rejected Edward's claim. Open warfare broke out in 1337 and with many, sometimes lengthy, intermissions would drag on until 1453. Spanning more than 117 years, this bloody contest for control of Normandy,

This map shows England and its possessions in France in 1154, almost two centuries prior to the opening of the Hundred Years' War.

the Aquitaine, the international wool trade, and the Crown of France came to be known as the Hundred Years' War.

APPANAGE FEUDALISM IN FRANCE

During the Middle Ages, the surest and easiest way for a man to make his fortune was to take it from someone else. The concept was nothing new; the Romans had used it in

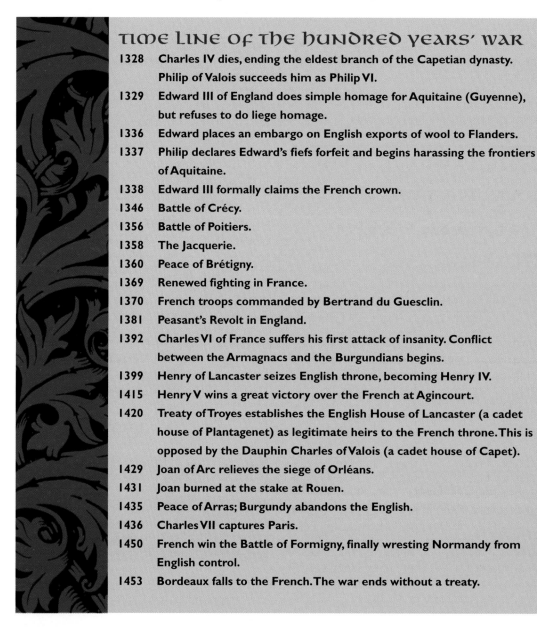

TIME LINE OF THE HUNDRED YEARS' WAR

1328   Charles IV dies, ending the eldest branch of the Capetian dynasty. Philip of Valois succeeds him as Philip VI.

1329   Edward III of England does simple homage for Aquitaine (Guyenne), but refuses to do liege homage.

1336   Edward places an embargo on English exports of wool to Flanders.

1337   Philip declares Edward's fiefs forfeit and begins harassing the frontiers of Aquitaine.

1338   Edward III formally claims the French crown.

1346   Battle of Crécy.

1356   Battle of Poitiers.

1358   The Jacquerie.

1360   Peace of Brétigny.

1369   Renewed fighting in France.

1370   French troops commanded by Bertrand du Guesclin.

1381   Peasant's Revolt in England.

1392   Charles VI of France suffers his first attack of insanity. Conflict between the Armagnacs and the Burgundians begins.

1399   Henry of Lancaster seizes English throne, becoming Henry IV.

1415   Henry V wins a great victory over the French at Agincourt.

1420   Treaty of Troyes establishes the English House of Lancaster (a cadet house of Plantagenet) as legitimate heirs to the French throne. This is opposed by the Dauphin Charles of Valois (a cadet house of Capet).

1429   Joan of Arc relieves the siege of Orléans.

1431   Joan burned at the stake at Rouen.

1435   Peace of Arras; Burgundy abandons the English.

1436   Charles VII captures Paris.

1450   French win the Battle of Formigny, finally wresting Normandy from English control.

1453   Bordeaux falls to the French. The war ends without a treaty.

building their empire—only to fall prey themselves to the Vandals, Goths, Huns, and Vikings, in turn. The sports of conquest, raid, and plunder in medieval Europe were kept partially in check by the protection afforded to those living under the feudal system. But by the fourteenth century, the feudal system had begun to break down in France thanks to the disjointed political structure of the country. France presented a particularly enticing target for territorial conquest, and the English fought

hard to take advantage of the situation. The reason the English were able to draw France so easily into the Hundred Years' War, and for the inordinate length of the conflict, lay in the peculiar practice of "appanage." Princes of the French royal family of Valois held large duchies and counties called appanages, which they ruled virtually independent of the king.

Appanages were originally intended to strengthen the royal family and administration by providing suitable status and income for a king's younger sons and, occasionally, royal daughters. In practice, however, the appanage princes fought to exclude the king's influence as much as possible. In their mutual maneuverings, one or another French prince was continually allying himself with the English, who were anxious to strengthen their grip on any, and all, French territory. At times it looked as if France would actually break up into quasi-independent principalities, many of them ruled by the English.

THE BATTLE OF CRÉCY (1346)

The first engagement of the war was a naval battle that took place at Sluys in 1340. Already a formidable naval power, the English fleet of 150 ships virtually wiped out the entire French fleet of 190 vessels in less than nine hours.

The same year Edward III landed his army in French-held Flanders and besieged Tournai but soon abandoned the siege as too difficult and struck a truce with King Philip of France. Having seen how vulnerable the French were when lured into the open field, or

Battle plan of the battle of Crécy in 1346 showing the disbursement of English and French troops. The masterful placement of English archers helped set the stage for decades of English victories over more traditional French tactics.

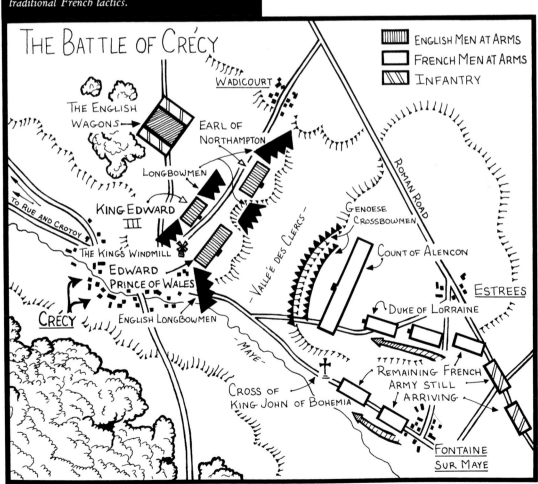

THE BATTLE OF CRÉCY

ENGLISH MEN AT ARMS
FRENCH MEN AT ARMS
INFANTRY

WADICOURT
THE ENGLISH WAGONS
EARL OF NORTHAMPTON
LONGBOWMEN
KING EDWARD III
TO RUE AND CROTOY
THE KING'S WINDMILL
EDWARD PRINCE OF WALES
CRÉCY
ENGLISH LONGBOWMEN
VALLÉE DES CLERCS
GENOESE CROSSBOWMEN
ROMAN ROAD
COUNT OF ALENCON
ESTREES
DUKE OF LORRAINE
MAYE
CROSS OF KING JOHN OF BOHEMIA
REMAINING FRENCH ARMY STILL ARRIVING
FONTAINE SUR MAYE

The armored knight of the Hundred Years' War period was equipped with a helmet with a visor that could be opened (here a style known as a "pig-faced bascinet") and a combination of plate and mail armor.

A member of the warrior nobility dressed in the height of military fashion during the latter half of the Hundred Years' War, complete with a pig-faced bascinet and a breastplate, in addition to arm and leg armor.

Here, common soldiers and archers are shown with no more armor than padded jackets to protect themselves, while the mounted knight is wearing a coat of brigadine (a padded jacket with small metal plates sewn between the layers of fabric) and an open-faced helmet known as a barbute.

Plate armor was now replacing mail armor and a knight wore a breastplate, arm and leg plates, and a heavy helmet complete with a visor that covered his face in combat. He wore a short surcoat emblazoned with his armorial device and fought with a lance (couched under his arm), a long sword, mace, and shield. Archers were protected by a mixture of mail shirts, jerkins of toughened leather, and steel caps; in addition to their bows and arrows, they carried swords, axes, and knives for close-quarter fighting. Foot soldiers primarily wielded a variety of pole weapons (halberds, partisans, glaives, pole axes, and such). The mounted knight was still considered the most formidable opponent on the field, and it was the task of the foot soldier to unhorse him.

the open water, the English continued to employ the tactic to great effect in the years to come. The six years following the Siege of Tournai were punctuated by intermittent periods of war separated by unstable truces. Full-blown hostilities reerupted with the infamous Battle of Crécy on 26 August 1346.

King Edward invaded Normandy with a force of some 25,000, composed of knights, men-at-arms, Welsh and Irish infantry, and a powerful force of archers equipped with long-bows. The king was accompanied by his eldest son, Edward, Prince of Wales, a lad of only sixteen who would be remembered by history as "the Black Prince." The King's army marched inland, captured Caen, and ravaged the countryside. In response, Philip VI of France raised an army of 60,000 and moved to meet the English. Anticipating the inevitable clash, Edward selected a battleground near the village of Crécy-en-Ponthieu and skillfully deployed his forces along a low rise sloping gently to the southeast. He chose the ground specifically for its terrain and the presence of a windmill on the summit of the hill, from which he could survey the battlefield.

Owing to previous loses of nearly 50 percent, the English now numbered only about 13,000 men, half of them archers. Having

divided his army into three divisions or "battles," Edward placed one on the right flank under the command of the Earls of Warwick and Oxford (with the Prince of Wales as titular commander), and one on the left flank under the Earls of Arundel and Northampton. The third "battle," kept some distance behind the others, was held in reserve under the personal command of the king. Horses and baggage train were placed far to the rear.

The nucleus of each division was a phalanx of dismounted men-at-arms. Each division was flanked by archers and a few small cannon known as "bombards"—among the earliest known uses of gunpowder artillery in field warfare.[9] To further impede the French, the English dug hundreds of small potholes in front of their ranks to break the legs of onrushing horses during cavalry charges.

In marked contrast to Edward's careful preparation, Philip's army blundered into battle with apparently little thought to tactical organization. Eager to get at the English, the French had marched in great haste, confident they would sweep the enemy from the field. Philip's massive force was composed of some 12,000 heavy cavalry, 17,000 light cavalry, 6,000 mercenary Genoese crossbowmen, and 25,000 peasant levies. Riding with the heavy

For 117 years, English armies marched across Normandy and Aquitaine, enforcing what they perceived as legitimate claims to these and other vast areas of French territory.

horse—the flower of French chivalry—were the kings of Bohemia and Majorca. The French were overconfident, but understandably so. Most medieval field battles had been a simple matter of ratios and numbers. The French outnumbered the English 60,000 to 13,000. French victory seemed assured.

On reaching the battleground, Philip attempted to halt his ponderous army for deployment, but when the front lines started to pull up, those in the rear continued to press forward. Mass confusion ensued. Each haughty lord and arrogant knight wanted his share of glory and was not going to be deterred by orders from his marshal or the king. As the French lines broke down in confusion, a thunderstorm began to lash the battlefield. When

the storm cleared, the sun broke through and shone on the backs of the English and directly into the eyes of the French.

Frustrated by his disorderly troops and the mercurial weather, Philip ordered his ranks of Genoese crossbowmen to open the battle. The mercenaries, however, complained they were unready for combat; the long march had wearied them and the sudden downpour had soaked and slackened their bowstrings. On hearing this complaint, the count of Alençon, King Philip's brother, commented sourly: "This is what we get by employing scoundrels who fail us when we most need them." The insult goaded the Genoese into action. Jean de Froissart records:

The Genoese set up a loud shout in order to frighten them, but the English remained quite still. They set up a second shout and advanced a little forward, but the English never moved. They shouted a third time, advancing with their crossbows presented, and begin to shoot [but their bolts, launched by slack strings, fell short]. The English archers then advanced one step forward [in order to pull back their strings which they had kept dry] and shot their arrows with such force and quickness that it seemed as if it snowed. When the Genoese felt these arrows pierce their arms, heads, and through their armor, they flung down their crossbows and ran back (Froissart, *Chronicles*).

Infuriated with the fleeing Genoese, King Philip commanded his forward knights to "Kill me those runaway rascals for they stop our path without reason!" Obediently, the glittering horsemen dashed into the ill-fated mercenaries and slaughtered them by the hundreds. The French chivalry held all foot soldiers, including archers and crossbowmen, in utter contempt and regarded them as unnecessary on the field of battle. In their code of war, only the knights counted.

Having ordered his knights to attack the crossbowmen, King Philip could no longer restrain them. The French horses charged towards the English, who continued to loose arrows thick and fast into the charging cavalry, bringing down knights and horses alike. More and more French horsemen barged forward, fighting their way through their own ranks to charge blindly into the devastating hail of arrows. As one knight after another crashed to the ground, Welsh and Irish foot soldiers armed with daggers slipped out of the English ranks and killed the horsemen as they lay stunned or wounded.

The fate of the aged and near-blind King John of Bohemia is exem-plary of the foolhardy sense of chivalry which permeated the French troops. "I pray you," he cried to his attendants, "to lead me into the thick of the fight that I may strike one good blow with this old sword of mine." Dutifully, the two knights secured their reins to those of their king's horse, and thus lashed together, all three rushed into the midst of battle—and were promptly killed.

Some knights managed to survive the fusillade of arrows and reach the division of the

The Welsh longbow, introduced into the English army early in the thirteenth century, quickly became one of the most effective weapons of medieval warfare. At the battle of Crécy over half of the English army was comprised of archers.

Prince of Wales, who found himself hard pressed by charging cavalry. A messenger rushed to King Edward to request assistance for the young prince, but the king refused to help, saying, "Let the boy win his spurs, for I am determined, if it pleases God, that the glory and honor of this day shall be his."

After sixteen futile charges over the course of eleven hours, the battered French finally quit the field in complete disorder. Edward forbade his men to pursue the fleeing enemy but held them in their ranks guarding their position until dawn. The Prince of Wales won his spurs right enough. The victory, however, could be attributed almost solely to the resolute bowmen of England. The crushing defeat stunned the French people: The very best of their chivalry had been wiped out by peasant archers! Mounted knights had been slaughtered by common foot soldiers! It was military and social heresy.

The French loses were enormous: More than 1,500 lords and knights and some 30,000 other ranks lay dead in the field. English casualties by comparison were extremely light: about 200 dead, including two knights. The battle of Crécy challenged the dictum that cavalry was the dominant, decisive factor on the battlefield. Dismounted troops supported by archers, if properly managed and deployed, could defeat heavy horsemen with simple economy. From that day—26 August 1346—feudalism, of which the mounted knight was the keystone, tottered slowly but surely toward oblivion.

Surprisingly, but predictably, the French learned very little from the terrible encounter at Crécy. The nobles persisted in the delusion that they had been vanquished by the English knights and men-at-arms. In fact, they even managed to convince themselves that the English surely had dismounted knights hidden among the foot soldiers, otherwise the French could never have been overwhelmed by them.

From 1347 to 1354, England and France observed a truce, while both nations were being devastated by the pestilence known as the Black Death, which cut down more than one-third of Europe's entire population.

THE BATTLE OF POITIERS (1356)

In 1355 hostilities resumed when Edward, the Black Prince of Wales, raided deep into southern France and returned to Bordeaux laden with the booty of hundreds of cities, towns, and villages. During the following year, he plundered his way through much of central France, until 17 September when he ran into a French army far larger than his own, commanded by the new king, John II, near the city of Poitiers.

Both sides prepared for battle. Edward chose an excellent position for a defensive stand, elevated ground with his flanks protected by vineyard walls and trenches, to which the only approach was a long, deep lane between hedgerows, so narrow that only four horsemen could ride abreast between them. Behind the hedgerows, Edward stationed massed contingents of archers. At the end of the lane, behind a thick hedge, he deployed dismounted knights and men-at-arms in three "battles" with archers on the flanks, similar in position to that used at Crécy.

The English army numbered about 12,000, of which some 8,000 were cavalry and 3,000 archers, the remaining 1,000 being foot soldiers and men-at-arms. This was an unusually high percentage of cavalry for the English at this time, but the English had been raiding their way through France, a job for which cavalry was preferable. The French force totaled about 35,000, including 16,000 horsemen and

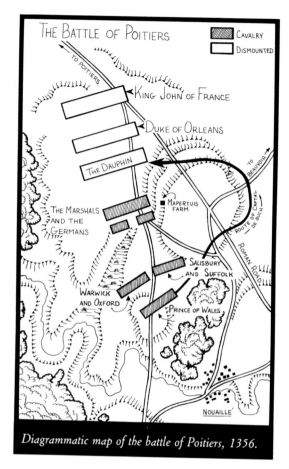

Diagrammatic map of the battle of Poitiers, 1356.

2,000 crossbowmen. With such a numerical advantage, the French once again felt sure of victory and were keen to join the battle. The English had virtually no provisions (some had not eaten for days), and the French could have easily played a waiting game and starved them into submission. But there was little martial glory in such mundane tactics.

Before the fight commenced, at midday on 19 September, Edward tried to negotiate a peaceful settlement with John, offering to give up all his plunder and prisoners, and pledge himself not to bear arms against France for seven years. In exchange he asked only for the free withdrawal of his hungry, outnumbered army. John refused the offer, demanding the prince's unconditional surrender. Edward declined and resolved to fight.

Believing that the English had triumphed at Crécy by dismounting their cavalry, John dismounted most of his horsemen and ordered them to cut down their twenty-foot lances to six foot. He deployed his dismounted knights and men-at-arms in three huge divisions, placing one behind the other, with two units of cavalry in front. He decided to launch a frontal attack through the narrow lane, in wave after wave, seemingly without regard for tactics or maneuver. He failed to see the huge disadvantage that dismounted knights weighted down by heavy armor would have trying to attack a strong position defended by foot soldiers.

The battle opened with a charge of 300 French horse. The English bowmen behind the hedges slaughtered the gleaming chivalry at short range with ease, their flashing "bodkin points" driving through horse and armor alike. Next came the dismounted knights commanded by the Dauphin. Despite ghastly losses inflicted by English bowmen, the French managed to press forward and engage the dismounted English knights in fierce combat. But the French, unaccustomed to fighting without their horses, tired quickly and were driven back. However, the English had been badly mauled.

The awful sight of the Dauphin's shattered division drained the fighting spirit of the Duke of Orléans' second division, which retreated in confusion before they came within range of the terrible rain of English arrows. The climax of the carnage came when John, a warrior king not easily intimidated, lead the final assault with the largest division of dismounted men, almost as numerous as the entire English army.

Although the French were exhausted from marching miles in their stifling armor, the English were also weary after hours of fierce fighting. Fearing that his soldiers could not withstand another determined attack, Edward

secondary contingent struck the French from behind. The Frenchmen wavered and began to quit the field. King John, with a hard core of his nobles, continued to fight on with his battle axe; Prince Philip stood by his side, warning him of danger: "Father, guard yourself on the right—guard yourself on the left!"

There was fierce competition amongst the English surrounding the king to capture him for his enormous ransom value. "Surrender, sire, or you are a dead man!" But John fought on, unwilling to yield to anyone of inferior rank. Froissart gives an account of his surrender:

> The King being hard pressed repeatedly asked, "Where is my cousin? Where is the Prince of Wales?" Then said a young knight, in French, "Sire, he is not here, but surrender yourself to me and I will lead you to him." Struck by the pure accent, the king asked, "Who are you?" The Frenchman replied, "I am Denis de Morbeque, a knight of Artois, but I serve the King of England because I have been banished from France." John then gave him his right-hand gauntlet, saying, "To you I surrender." And he and his son were conducted to the Prince of Wales (Froissart, Chronicles).

So ended the battle of Poitiers. The French had suffered yet another shattering defeat. English losses were in the region of 2,000 dead and wounded, while nearly 25,000 French knights and men-at-arms lay dead. Nearly as many were taken prisoner, including many lords, nobles, and the king. The Prince of Wales, chivalrous in the extreme, treated his royal captive with great respect.

John remained a captive, enjoying regal comfort and company, in the palace of Savoy until he was released on payment of three million gold crowns at the Peace of Bretigny in 1360. Meanwhile, France was plunged into

Sent into battle in contingents of hundreds, or even thousands, English longbowmen provided supporting fire for heavy cavalry and quickly became the scourge of the medieval battlefield.

decided to commit his reserve of 400 mounted knights to a charge, taking the added precaution of sending a body of horsemen and archers to hit the French in the rear.

"Advance, banners, in the name of God and St. George!" echoed through the ranks as Edward led the gallop. The horsemen collided with King John's division with such impact that (legend has it) the crash was heard in Poitiers, seven miles away. As the two forces slashed, hacked, and stabbed in blind fury, Edward's

misery. The routed soldiery of Poitiers turned into free companies of bandits while the nobles held prisoner by the English purchased their ransom by extortive taxation which drove the peasantry of France into nearly universal revolt.

With the Peace of Bretigny, the King of England waived his claim on the French crown and the Duchy of Normandy. But he retained the Duchy of Aquitaine—which included Gascony, Guienne, Poictou, and Saintonge—not as a fief to the French crown, but in full sovereignty. His most recent conquest, the port of Calais, was also to remain an English possession.

THE BATTLE OF AGINCOURT (1415)

During the next half century, internal problems and a series of near revolutions kept England from pressing its claims on French territory. All this was to change, however, when the ambitious young Henry V came to the throne in 1413. In August 1415, he landed in Normandy with an army of 12,000 men.

Henry besieged and captured the town of Harfleur. The siege, though successful, cost Henry dearly. The majority of his knights and men-at-arms were killed, wounded, or fell prey to disease. The only forces that remained relatively unscathed in the siege were the archers who always worked from a distance. The English now numbered about 6,000, of which 5,000 were archers. Henry decided to march to Calais where his army could spend the winter in recuperation awaiting reserves from England. The French became aware of Henry's plan and decided to cut off his army of sick and wounded survivors before they could reach Calais. Near the castle of Agincourt, the weakened and hungry English were confronted by a French force of 30,000 under Charles d'Albret, constable of France.

The Battle of Agincourt is so impressed on our minds (as much by Shakespeare's play as by history) that it clouds the real nature of the fighting. The circumstances that led to the battle were particular: The French tried to intercept the English army on their way to Calais, relying again on superiority of numbers to give them victory. The English were not seeking a battle, but once found, they were not about to shun it. The open field proved to be a considerable advantage for the English because it allowed them to use massed discharges of arrows. Open-field fighting allowed full use of

At the battle of Agincourt in 1415, English long-bowmen opened the hostilities with a fusillade of 72,000 arrows, fired in the first ninety seconds of battle, cutting the French army to ribbons.

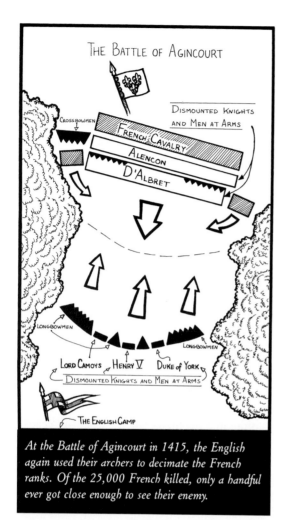

THE BATTLE OF AGINCOURT

CROSSBOWMEN

DISMOUNTED KNIGHTS
AND MEN AT ARMS

FRENCH CAVALRY

ALENCON

D'ALBRET

LONGBOWMEN

LONGBOWMEN

LORD CAMOYS   HENRY V   DUKE OF YORK

DISMOUNTED KNIGHTS AND MEN AT ARMS

THE ENGLISH CAMP

At the Battle of Agincourt in 1415, the English again used their archers to decimate the French ranks. Of the 25,000 French killed, only a handful ever got close enough to see their enemy.

lines, each unit flanked by strong bodies of archers.

Each bowman carried a sharpened stake which he stuck in the ground before him at an angle (in the manner of a *chevaux de frise* or picket), its spike set to impale enemy horsemen. It is said that Henry focused the desperation of his brave bowmen by telling them that the French had vowed to ruin them as archers forever by cutting off the middle fingers of any who were captured.

Constable d'Albret, commander of the French forces, also formed his men into three divisions, but he placed them one behind the other. The first two divisions were composed of dismounted knights and men-at-arms; the third of horsemen, with crossbowmen placed on the flanks and in between the divisions. This time d'Albret wisely decided to stand his ground and defend, letting the English attack and destroy themselves, as the French had done at Crécy and Poitiers. For several hours both armies waited for the other to advance.

Henry, realizing what the French commander had in mind, decided to provoke the enemy into impetuous action. He advanced his army half a mile in formation, then called them to a halt. The archers replanted their sharpened stakes in front of them. The sight of the hated English so near and so few in number excited the passion of the French chivalry to the boiling point. They could no longer contain themselves. Throwing discipline and caution to the wind, the first division crashed forward, while contingents of mounted knights on the flanks leveled their lances and charged.

The ploughed and sodden fields deprived the cavalry of speed and the heavy horsemen moved in slow motion, lurching and sinking in the water-logged ground. In their wake, the knights on foot struggled through the churning sea of mud. Once again English archers poured their arrows into the closely packed,

this tactic, and when English fought English later in the century, during the Wars of the Roses, both sides employed it to the near exclusion of siege warfare. The French, on the other hand, did not employ archers in this way, preferring to work from behind fortifications from which they often rashly emerged.

The two armies faced each other across a mile of freshly ploughed fields situated between two large woods. The fields were thoroughly sodden by a week of heavy rain. The open frontage between the woods measured about 1,200 yards. Henry adopted a defensive position similar to that of his predecessors at Crécy and Poitiers: The dismounted men-at-arms formed into three "battles" facing the enemy

sluggish enemy and inflicted horrible damage. Of the 1,200 French horsemen, not more than 120 ever reached the bowmen's spiked barricade, from which the horses recoiled in fear, throwing their riders to the ground.

Hundreds of wounded, screaming steeds rushed to and fro, stampeding over French foot soldiers, causing confusion and panic. Those few knights who survived the rain of arrows and actually reached the English line were cut down by dismounted men-at-arms and archers; the latter having a "savage appearance this day. Many had stripped themselves naked; others had bared their arms and breasts that they might exercise their limbs with more ease and execution." In addition to bow and arrows, each archer carried an axe or sword for close combat. Light and agile, the bowmen pounced on their heavily armored opponents and beat on them "as though they were smiths hammering upon anvils."

The French attacked again and again until they were ruined. The entire battle lasted only three hours. The French suffered appalling losses. Froissart's *Chronicle* records:

When some of the enemy's van were slain, those behind pressed over the dead, and others again falling on them, they were immediately put to death; and in three places near Henry's banner so large was a pile of corpses that the English stood on the heaps, which exceeded a man's height, and butchered their adversaries below with their swords and axes.

Henry V was continually in the thick of the fight and under personal attack, twenty French knights having sworn on the cross of their swords to capture or kill him. Henry presented a provocatively singular target: "His helmet was of polished steel, surmounted by a crown sparkling with jewels, and his surcoat emblazoned with the Arms of England and France." At one point he was stunned by a blow from a mace and found himself confronted by the Duke d'Alençon, who had already killed the Duke of York while fighting his way to the king. D'Alençon struck the crown from Henry's head and lifted his sword for a more effectual blow, but the king's attendants cut him down and slew him.

The French lost 25,000, most of them nobles and men-at-arms, and 1,000 more were taken prisoner. Constable d'Albret, who cannot be blamed for a defeat brought about by the hasty, impassioned chivalry, was among those killed. English losses have been estimated as low as "fewer than a hundred" to as high as 1,600. What can be said with certainty is that English casualties were considerably less than those of the French, despite being outnumbered nearly five to one. It is said that as the massed English archers marched off the field past the broken remnants of the French army, they graphically demonstrated that their middle fingers were not only still intact but perfectly operational. Agincourt was yet another damaging blow to the reputation of the ponderous, imperious, and inefficient armored knight.

The war dragged on in a sporadic and haphazard manner. The decisive field battles illustrated here were short lived victories. The French eventually learned that if they were to successfully defend their country, they had to protect themselves and rely on their castles. Many sieges would take place in an attempt to rout the French from their fortresses, but they would be to no avail. In the decades following Agincourt, the war went almost exclusively to the disadvantage of the English who, as an invading force, were usually forced to fight on the offensive. In July 1453 came the battle of Castillon, in which the English launched an attack of dismounted men-at-arms and pikemen, flanked by archers, against an entrenched position protected by gunpowder artillery.

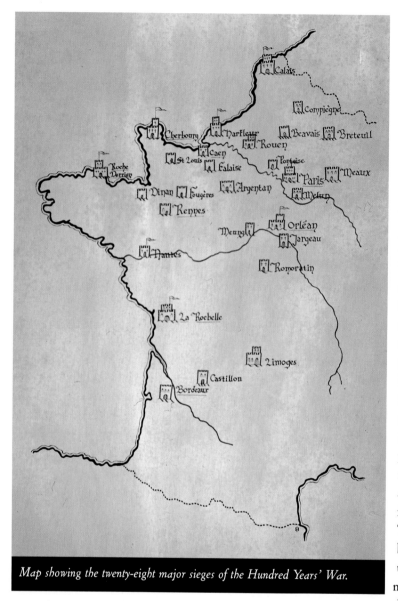

Map showing the twenty-eight major sieges of the Hundred Years' War.

There are two factors of primary importance in examining these events. First, the English tactic of luring the French out of their castles to engage them in the open field speaks to the effectiveness of castles. Secondly, it is clear that the nature of warfare and the demographics of armies were in the process of change. The English relied heavily on artillery (archers in the beginning, though gradually incorporating gunners) whereas the French relied on the traditional heavy cavalry and castle fortification. In the final analysis, the English concept of a "mobile army" prevailed. Modern armies rely almost exclusively on artillery, rather than fortification and entrenchment. The English, who had brought castle architecture to its pinnacle of development under Edward I, were the first to revise their armies specifically to function in the open field. But as Sir Isaac Newton was to observe centuries later: "For every action there is an equal and opposite reaction." Inevitably, advancements in fortification techniques inspired equally improved siege tactics. The remainder of this book will concern itself with the various means employed in attempts to overwhelm these great fortresses during the closing years of the Hundred Years' War.

After the cannon had pounded the English to a standstill, the French counterattacked and swept the enemy from the field. This decisive victory, which stilled the ghosts of Crécy, Poitiers, and Agincourt, was followed by the French capture of Bordeaux in October of 1453, thus bringing an end to the Hundred Years' War. Of all the wide English conquests in France, there remained only the Channel Islands and the seaport of Calais, the latter being lost in 1558.

Chapter Four

SETTING THE STAGE

Siege Theory and Tactical Approaches

When two nobles quarrel, the poor man's thatch goes up in flames....
—anonymous, fourteenth century

We have seen how the fields of France were bathed in blood as noblemen rode forth from their castles to engage the English in the open field. Their strategy may have been blunt and unsophisticated, but it provided ample opportunity for heroic bravado and daring-do. More to the point, it was a tactic by which the siege could be avoided altogether. Military leaders disliked sieges because they kept hundreds, or even thousands, of soldiers in one location for months and sometimes years. Haughty, independent knights also hated the prospect of a siege because opportunities for elaborate cavalry formations and personal acts of valor simply did not exist as long as castle walls protected their enemy. Far worse for the knights, most of the day-to-day fighting in a siege was conducted by archers, engineers, miners, and mercenaries, all of whom were uncouth commoners. In short, sieges were not battles of glory; they were grueling contests of cunning, patience, and nerve. In this chapter we will examine the complicated issues of why and how sieges were undertaken as part of the larger framework of medieval warfare.

Medieval field battles were a straightforward test of strength. The opposing forces engaged each other in face-to-face combat and used their particular strength, whether it be sheer numbers or improved technology, to battle it out until one side was driven from the field. A siege, on the other hand, more closely resembled a game of chess: Numerical strength was certainly important, as are the number of pieces each player has on the chessboard, but of far greater importance in determining the outcome was the position and interrelation of the pieces. As any chess player knows, more kings are captured with pawns than with knights.

It seems remarkable, in retrospect, that the bloody carnage of a field battle was preferred over a well-orchestrated siege by attackers and defenders alike. Logically, mounting a defense from a well-protected position should have been preferable to facing an opponent on the open battlefield, but the warlords of the period seem to have disagreed. We can never completely understand the thought processes of the medieval mind, but some indication can be glimpsed by the thoughts recorded by warriors of the period. Bertrand de Burn writes:

I love to see a lord when he is the first to advance on horseback, armed and fearless, thus encouraging his men to valiant service; then, when the fray has begun, each must be ready to follow him willingly, because no one is held in esteem until he has given and received blows. We shall see clubs and swords, gaily colored helmets and shields shattered and spoiled… and many great vassals all together receiving great blows, by reason of which many horses will wander riderless….

Once he has started fighting, no noble knight thinks of anything but breaking heads and arms—better a dead man than a live one who is useless. I tell you, neither in eating, drinking nor sleeping do I find what I find when I hear the shout "At them!" from both sides, and the neighing of horses in the confusion, or the cry "Help! Help!", or when I see great and small fall on the grass of the ditches, or when I espy dead men who still have pennoned lances in their ribs.

Equally ardent is Jean de Bevil:

It is a joyous thing, a war. You love your comrade so much in war. When you see that your quarrel is just, and your blood is fighting well, tears rise to your eyes. A great sweet feeling of loyalty and of pity fills your heart on seeing your friend so valiantly exposing his body. And then you are prepared to go and die or live with him, and for love not to abandon him. And out of that there arises such a delight, that he who has not experienced it is not fit to say what delight is. Do you think that a man who does that fears death? Not at all, for he feels so strengthened, so elated, that he does not know where he is. Truly he is afraid of nothing.

Despite the fact that sieges were frequently resolved with a very low number of casualties, the brutal, decisive carnage of the battlefield seems to have been peculiarly attractive. This marked preference for the battlefield aside, medieval history is filled with sieges.

In most cases, castles and fortified towns that underwent sieges were never directly in the path of an oncoming army. Why then would an army go out of its way, at considerable expense, to lay siege to a fortification which they might well destroy once it was captured—especially when sieges were so obviously unpopular? The answer has to do with the very nature of castles and their role in the overall concept of medieval warfare. Undoubtedly, medieval military strategists knew that no matter how much fun hacking each other to bits might be, if a war was to be won, the castles, which were each region's political and military center, had to be captured and controlled.

one simply by its presence. To protect the territory around them, castles were sited at such logical places as fording points in rivers, the entrance to valleys, near bridges, close to towns, or near seaports. To protect themselves, they were situated where they could command one or more valleys, provide excellent observation posts, and be as difficult as possible to approach and capture.

> By the fourteenth century, armies of mercenaries were already beginning to replace peasant levies in many European armies, including those of England and France.

CASTLE STRATEGY

Over the course of a thousand years of tribal and district warfare, virtually every point of strategic importance in Europe, the British Isles and the Middle East had been located, fortified, and probably defended. Traces of these defensive ditches, embankments, or ambushes still exist throughout the western world. Nevertheless, they belong to a different defensive concept than the castle. They were only constructed to check and hinder the invader, and represent a simple tactical device that protected the defender while forcing the aggressor to fight at a disadvantage.

Castle strategy belongs to a larger concept of warfare. The aim of every castellan was to place his fortification at a point where it would either enhance a natural obstacle or create an entirely new

However, there were particular liabilities involved in siting castles in lofty places, and these had to be guarded against. When a castle was situated in mountainous country, getting food to its garrison might be difficult, and thus, under the right circumstances, a light siege, maintained over an extended period of time, would suffice to starve out a garrison. Another liability was one which many garrisons still face today: lonely, boring, inaccessible places are bad for morale. Such places earn a reputation as being more of a punishment than an assignment.

Surprisingly, many of the most strategically important castles were built on rather accessible terrain. In the hands of an ingenious strategist—and medieval Europe had plenty of them—flat or even hollow ground could prove to be the most formidable sites of all. Most low-lying ground in the Middle Ages was marshy, a feature often used to keep back the freight wagons, heavily armored cavalry, and massive siege engines that were an integral part of every medieval army. Castles positioned in almost any terrain could be used to great effect as staging points for mounting flanking attacks on an invading force.

For the remainder of the book, we will create and examine a fictional siege led by fictional commanders as part of a larger invasion force. We will create a siege, rather than examine an actual historical one, so that we can examine all of the facets of siege warfare in depth, including peculiarities of terrain, constraints of time and money, and the personal strategies of individual commanders. To understand just how difficult it was to mount a siege, we must also place it within an overall invasion plan.

Asssume that the English are about to invade an area of French-held Normandy to enforce some political claim or other during an episode of the Hundred Years' War. Certainly, over the 117-year course of the war, such events took place frequently. In our fictional siege, the English force, planning to invade a particular rural province of Normandy, has an army of 16,000 men. The English are confident of victory because the area targeted for invasion has a small population and can reasonably be expected to raise an army of no more than 10,000. Now that we have established the intent of the English, let us see just how much planning is necessary to mount such a campaign. Only in Hollywood do we find knights leaping into their saddles, waving their swords, and galloping off on campaign. The image may be exciting, but launching a war takes considerably more preparation.

Demographics of the Besieging Force

Only the richest monarchs could afford to maintain a permanent fighting force greater than a personal guard of a few hundred men. French and Burgundian attempts to create standing armies proved incredibly unpopular among those whose taxes paid for them. Therefore, when an army was raised, it was usually assembled for the occasion. Detailed contracts were drawn up between monarchs and professional recruiters. The contracts established fixed rates of pay; rules of conduct, reward, and punishment; training requirements; and supplies of equipment and food stuffs. That was, at least, the idea. Although it often broke down, this type of system was necessary for an army hoping to fight a successful campaign, or even to march to its objective without starving or breaking up.

During the campaign of Edward, the Black Prince, into France (culminating with the Battle of Poitiers), a knight was paid two shillings a day, a man-at-arms a shilling a day, a mounted archer six pence a day, and the humble foot soldier two pence a day. "Bannerets," veteran knights of proven valor who directed contingents in the field and served as staff officers to the commanders, were paid four shillings a day. By comparison, a master carpenter in England received three pence a day, and a reaper two pence. Land could be rented at four pence an acre a year. Soldiers on campaign had the opportunity to enrich themselves by collecting plunder and demanding ransom for wealthy prisoners. Naturally, common soldiers would never be allowed to hold noblemen as their prisoners (nor would any nobleman, preferring death to dishonor, surrender to a common foot soldier), but the soldiers would receive the lion's share of any plunder.

By the fourteenth century, hiring professional soldiers (mercenaries), led by experienced captains, had proved far more effective than pressing untrained amateurs into service. Mercenaries could be hired as often and in as great a number as necessary and could be discharged when no longer needed. But professional soldiers expected to be paid, well and regularly, and they would desert if their pay was not forthcoming.

A popular axiom among medieval military commanders may well have been "supplies cost money, the dead cost nothing." Commanders and recruiters attempted to negotiate contracts so that neither mercenaries nor regular soldiers were paid until the term of service was complete. In this way, desertion was discouraged, and because a significant percentage of the men would be dead before pay day, they would not require payment. Conversely, the mercenaries would attempt to negotiate the contract in such a way that they were paid on a weekly or even daily basis. Experienced mercenary captains understood that if a commander spent money to keep sol-diers in the field, he would be a bit more reticent to send them on a suicide mission. Furthermore, if the hired soldiers decided to desert, they would have some payment in their purses for services rendered.

While contracts were being negotiated and drafted, tacticians and military advisors would devise an overall campaign strategy. Medieval strategists used the observations of Vegetius, a tactician of the later Roman Empire, as a sort of field service pocket manual. By the fifteenth century, *Regulae Bellorum Generales* (Vegetius's treatise) was available in French, English, and Latin. Vegetius believed in hard training and meticulous preparation. He wrote: "The better the troops of a garrison are trained and accustomed to discipline, the less problem one will have with them during battle.... Only a few men are brave by nature—good training increases their numbers." He also believed that a good general would engage in battle only when he was certain of victory.

Following the advice of Vegetius, a commander would weigh the chances of success against a dozen different factors before making any decisive moves. State craft, including war, was like a subtle, never-ending game of chess, played for the highest possible stakes.

When a medieval army set off on campaign, it could not simply plunge blindly into unknown territory. Merchants, pilgrims, wagon drivers, and soldiers all traveled far and frequently; many people could be found who knew the countryside over which the army must pass, and others along the way knew the roads in their own region. At least some of these people could be convinced to provide directions for an invading army for the right price, or through forceful persuasion. Most military leaders had their espionage departments to

provide such information; one writer suggested, "A prince should spend a third of his revenue on spies." Bribes, gifts, and promises were everyday weapons of political warfare. An agent with up-to-date knowledge of who could be influenced, or "turned," and who could not was a valuable asset.

supply lines

Once an overall strategy had been devised, the invaders were faced with the arduous task of assembling massive siege trains, including engineers, workmen, and supplies to sustain their campaign for months while they were in enemy territory.

Some idea of how vast and complex an

Here we see castle guards providing rudimentary training to the conscripted peasants who will help to defend the fortress.

undertaking it was to organize a major invasion can be found in the *Book of Armes and of Chyvalrye* written in French in 1408 and 1409 by Christine de Pisan and eventually translated into English in 1489, after the Hundred Years' War had safely come to an end.[10] Under the heading "Of Leyenge of a Syege and of Sawtyngys of Fortresses," she listed all the arms and equipment needed by an attacking force over a six-month siege:

The best time to attack is at harvest, when the attackers can deprive the defenders of vital supplies and benefit themselves. Proclamations must be made in the surrounding villages forbidding trade with the besieged, and encouraging it with the besiegers. Vast quantities of timbers, wagons, horses and oxen are necessary, and if moving by water then barges, boats, and a crane to unload them.

A barricade must be constructed completely surrounding the fortress, nearly one and a half miles long, built of 540 wooden panels 14 ft. long by 12 ft. high with gates and wooden towers. A barn 144 ft. by 48 ft. must be built for the horse-powered flour mills and other equipment. Over 3,000 carpenters and laborers should be recruited, many of them also archers, with rope makers, wheelwrights, and turners. 30,000 lbs. of gunpowder, 2,200 stones, 6,000 lbs. of lead, 200,000 crossbow quarrels, and 1,200 pavises. Double ladders "wyth grete hokes of yron that shall a grype the batellments", 1,000 shovels, 200 lanterns, barrels with locks and keys, tallow to lubricate wheels...

The fact that this list goes on and on should come as no surprise. While medieval chroniclers quoted figures to impress rather than to convey exact figures, account books were kept by a different sort of person and therefore provide us with muster rolls and ration lists which help to find the truth about the scope of medieval invasions. In a chronicle, a statement of "60,000 of the enemy perished" may simply mean "a lot," but in a muster roll, "60,000 arrows" listed as supplies probably means 60,000 arrows.

To illustrate the extent of preparation and supplies required for a lengthy siege, examine the following passage concerning Edward III's march from Rheims to Paris in 1360 as recorded by Jean de Froissart:

You ought to know that the King of England and the rich brought with them on their carts tents, pavilions, mills, cooking ovens, horse smithies and everything needful. And to furnish this they brought along quite six thousand carts, each with four good strong cart horses brought out of England. And on the carts they had many boats, so cleverly made of boiled leather that it was surprising to see them. They could carry three men so as to float on even the biggest lake or fishpond and fish at will. Thus they were quite comfortable in Lent—that is to say the Lords and people of standing. But the common folk had to make do with what they could get. Furthermore the king personally had thirty mounted falconers with birds and sixty couples of strong hounds and the same number of greyhounds. With these he went hunting or fishing every day according to his fancy. Many of the noble and wealthy also had their dogs and birds like the king....

Now add to this impressive list the amount of food and drink, not to mention storage and shelter, for the foot soldiers, and cavalry (with their horses), engineers, miners, sappers, camp followers, boys, and baggage necessary to provision our hypothetical English invasion force of

16,000 soldiers, and the logistics become positively nightmarish.

LOGISTICS AND MOVEMENT

Once a commander had assembled thousands of men along with all of the associated equipment and supplies, the next obstacle was moving them into, and through, enemy territory. When a medieval army went into the field, it faced the same problems as any army did before the advent of motorized transport. Assuming the enemy was going to make foraging as difficult as possible, enough basic food and drink for several weeks had to be carried on pack animals or in wagons and carts pulled by horses or oxen—which also had to be fed. Arrows and crossbow bolts by the hundreds of thousands, spare bows and strings, artillery, powder and shot, armorers and their equipment, tents and camping kit, tools of all kinds, materials for sieges and bridge building, clothing, bedding, medical supplies, the personal gear of the officers' households—ton upon ton of cumbersome impedimenta had to be transported, much of it packed in barrels and locked trunks.

The wagons and draft animals, in turn, demanded even more wagons to haul the fodder, tools, forges, smiths, wheelwrights, and ferriers that kept them fed and in working order. Transport had to be provided for the men who kept the transport rolling; for those who pitched and struck the camp, and packed and unpacked all the barrels and bales; and for the clerks and quartermasters who noted, stored, and issued it all, and made sure it arrived in the right place at the right time. To make transportation even more problematic, wagons and drivers were only occasionally part of the military establishment, more often they were civilians, either hired or pressed into service as needed.

A German source from the end of the fifteenth century lists the number of wagons needed to move an army of 15,000 (very close to the size of our own imaginary English force of 16,000). Six hundred and fifty wagons are needed to move supplies for 12,000 foot soldiers and an additional 300 wagons for 3,000 cavalry. An infantry of this size, marching three men abreast and accompanied by 3,000 horsemen riding in pairs, and allowing 19 feet for draft animals between each of the 950 wagons, gives our army a length of 14.5 miles while it is on the march. If the entire entourage attempted to camp together at night and move out in order the next morning, the head of the column

Provision wagons carrying arrows, bows, armor, parts for siege engines, tents for the noblemen, cooking pots, and all the other gear and equipment necessary to run a military campaign, traveled much slower than mounted knights, or even marching soldiers. Their presence could slow the advance of an invading army to a crawl.

Always anxious to catch the French in the open field where they could use their longbowmen and superior battle tactics to the greatest advantage, the English were frustrated when the French chose to use their numerous castles to their best advantage.

would reach the next night's campsite before the rear of the column could even set off.

The speed of an army's march naturally depended on the condition of the roads, the season, and the weather. Armies were occasionally capable of moving surprisingly fast, which argues for good organization and well-maintained roads. The Black Prince's great raid from Bordeaux to the Channel coast and back in October and November of 1355 averaged more than 9 miles a day for over two months, in which time they covered 560 miles—impressive for an army which assaulted many towns en route and was laden with booty.[11] Research indicates that crusading armies covered a daily average of between 6 to 10 miles on very long marches.[12] The organization and execution of

such massive undertakings was so complex that we could analyze it *ad infinitum, ad nauseum*. It may be more instructive, however, to return to our hypothetical model.

Assuming that the English moved 16,000 men, 3,000 war horses, 3,800 draft animals, 950 wagons, and all the assorted goods, food, and equipment across the English Channel without undue incident, the commanders then organize their army into a train and begin making their way inland. Their advance proceeds relatively unchecked at the rate of nine miles a day, because the chosen route through the farmland of Normandy has no natural obstacles, such as mountains or river crossings. The English do not, in fact, encounter any problems until their column moves toward a broad valley laying between two ranges of steep hills. At least part of the reason the English have made such steady progress is because they are purposefully being drawn deep into the country so that the French can choose their own battleground.

As the English approach the valley, it rapidly becomes apparent that all is not well. Much of the valley floor is either bog land or marsh, and the usually rich crop land of Normandy has been burnt off in midseason. The few villages they find have been abandoned or put to the torch. Sensing a trap, the English commander sends scouts ahead to reconnoiter and calls the army to a halt. The next day the returning scouts report that the valley is easily six miles wide and thirty miles long and the ranges of hills bordering it are steep and heavily wooded. The wetland farming communities that once filled the valley have all been deserted and, in many cases, destroyed.

High in the hills, on opposite sides of the valley, are two castles and two more guard the edge of the marsh, one of which is nearly impossible to reach because it is surrounded by water. For the English, the only practical path to their ultimate target looks less and less inviting. The moment they pass between the castles, their retreat, though perhaps not prevented, will become slow and hazardous and their line of communication will undoubtedly be cut. Knights and common soldiers alike would prefer to fight their way in and slaughter the French in the process, but at the moment, there is no way to get at them. There is also no way of knowing where or how many French troops there may be in the area.

Because the main danger to their enterprise now comes from the garrisons sheltered in the castles, the English must estimate the time and number of men required to besiege and, hopefully, neutralize them. The castles are well situated to protect themselves and their valley, and the defenders have the considerable advantage of cover. The English commander must estimate whether the garrisons are large or small and whether the main force of the French army is camped on the plains ahead of

him, waiting for him to divide his forces in a series of sieges so that they can swoop in and slaughter the separated units. Or could these castles be no more than decoys to draw him forward until his forces are surrounded in inhospitable country?

There is no sure way to know if there are 20 men or 2,000 men in each of the castles, but the risk of leaving four castles intact and behind his column is too great a threat. The English must immobilize them even if they cannot capture them. Assuming there are no more than 400 men in each castle, the English commander determines that he will need to employ a five to one numerical superiority of manpower to take the castles. He detaches units of 1,800 men each to the two hill forts and two more units of 2,200 men each to the castles on the valley floor. The deployment immediately creates supply and logistical problems. The castles have already done their job. Without being directly involved in either attack or defense, these four castles have effectively reduced the size of the invading force by half.

The main body of the English force is now down to 8,000 men, who are trying to live off the burned and depleted country to preserve their limited supplies. If they run into any more tactical problems, they could find themselves facing a foe with superior numbers fighting on familiar ground. Although a medieval strategist would not have known the term, this concept is now known as "defense in depth." It is a difficult equation, but the medieval castle made full use of it.

But castles were not only designed for defensive purposes; they performed equally well as a mechanism for attack. At some point, every advancing army needs to stop and regroup, to dig in and prepare for counterattack. The castle was a refinement of the tactic of digging-in. Castles provided a network for defense and a springboard for attack. They were armories and

Provisions, supplies, and building materials are hauled into the fortress, and hurried repairs are made to the aging defenses before the English can begin to mount a siege.

Arrows, crossbow bolts, and stones, along with buckets of pitch and quick-lime are hauled to the battlements along the castle walls. The French are determined to drive back the small English army that is on its way to besiege their castle.

ordinance depots, observation points and forward positions, headquarters and homes. They provided an observation post, storehouse, recovery center, and residence. They were the most closely integrated form of military and domestic life the world has ever seen.

For mutual protection, most castles were located within a day's march of at least one other castle. Such proximity allowed them to provide cover for each other and, if necessary, send reinforcements or mount diversionary attacks. The fact that castles were personal possessions that could be parceled out among invading noblemen gave the defenders a special urgency in holding and maintaining their position and cooperating with each other in times of hostility.

We have seen how immense an undertaking it was for an army to mount an invasion force, but how difficult was it for an individual castle to prepare for the possibility of an enemy siege?

THE BESIEGED

Unless a castle was likely to be directly in the path of an advancing army, most of the garrison would probably be mobilized to join the main body of their army to repel the invasion. Because nearly all of their fighting force could be called away in time of war, castles, as we have seen, were designed to remain defensible with a relatively small force. During surprise attacks a well-designed castle manned by only a few dozen soldiers could withstand a concerted attack by an entire wing of an army. Conversely, too many defending troops could actually reduce a castle's efficiency and its ability to withstand a siege.

In the case of our model siege, forward scouts return to the French castle, warning that the English have dispatched a contingent of

between two and three thousand men to subdue them. The castellan would then make any preparations necessary to give the English a properly frustrating welcome. As the war approaches, the prudent castellan keeps his garrison hard at work. Specific preparations vary widely from castle to castle, but basic defensive procedures are fairly universal.

The castellan appoints sentinels and lookouts to operate within and without the castle. He then begins defensive preparations by calling up a levy of all available manpower from the surrounding district. Regular troops are put in charge of the peasant levies, which are divided into work parties assigned to carry out defensive measures. While one group brings crossbow quarrels, arrows, and disassembled siege weapons out of storage, another moves buckets of pitch, water, and quicklime along with piles of timbers and iron pry bars to the wall walks. Women and old men are set to work weaving heavy wicker mats that can be lowered to protect the walls from the effects of battering rams.

The balance between manpower and supplies is critical if the garrison is to survive a prolonged siege. If there are too many defenders, or they are under siege too long, they run the risk of facing starvation before relief can arrive. To reduce food consumption, all nonessential personnel is ordered out of the castle. To further prevent depletion of precious supplies, sanctuary is routinely denied to refugees fleeing the approaching war, with the exception of members of the clergy, noblemen, and knights whose own property has been overrun by the advancing army. Peasants are more easily replaced than lost land or castles, and they were frequently caught between the approaching invaders and the holder of the local castle who was, in theory at least, their protector.

Jean de Froissart, writing of the Battle of

With repair work nearly completed, all non-combatants are driven from the castle to stretch existing food supplies for as long as possible. The peasants, driven out yet again, have no alternative but to return to their homes and pray that the approaching English will simply ignore them.

Catching sight of the approaching English army, the peasants flee back to the castle and beg sanctuary, but their pleas fall on deaf ears.

To display their determination to take land and castle alike, the English knights pursue the peasants to the very gates of the French castle.

I n the First Crusade, when the Turks besieged the Crusaders in the Castle of Xerigordo near Nicea and cut off their water supply, the beleaguered Christians suffered terrific hardships, drinking their horses' blood and each others' urine, and burying themselves in damp earth in hope of absorbing some of the moisture. After eight days without water, the Christians surrendered and were killed or sold as slaves.

Poitiers in 1356, describes such a situation:

The chase endured to the gates; where there were many slain and beaten down... for they ... closed their gates and would suffer none to enter. Wherefore in the street before the gate was horrible murder....

The hope of every castle facing a siege was that the king and the main body of his army would arrive and offer speedy relief, but war is unpredictable, and so are kings, and the worst must be prepared for. Consequently, on receiving word that the English are headed in their direction, our French garrison calls in all available, experienced troops from the surrounding area and orders supplies of artillery, ammunition, and arrows. While a group of engineers assembles the siege machines which are brought up from the cellars, wooden hoardings are built on the parapet, and fortifications are repaired or improved as much as possible in the time available. Teams of less skilled workers clear debris out of the ditches and moat surrounding the castle. The walls in some sections of the ditch are recut to make them steeper and more precarious.

A party of knights is sent to gather all available food supplies from the villages controlled by the castle. Any produce or livestock that cannot be moved to the castle, along with all crops in the field, are either burnt or slaughtered. The peasants' permission is not asked, and compensation for their losses will not be given. After the stores have been gathered at the castle, the commander determines a ration scale. Provisions of livestock and food, for both men and horses, are brought in.

Some castles were large enough to warehouse a year's supply of basic foodstuffs. The relatively small size of a fourteenth-century garrison often meant that in a prolonged siege, the assailants, rather than the besieged, could be confronted with a supply problem. A well-supplied garrison of sixty men could frequently hold out against an attacking force twenty times its number. Feeding 60 men from a well-stocked granary supplemented by cattle, pigs, and chickens, was far easier than feeding 1,200 men from a war-ravaged countryside.

But ours is not a small garrison of 60 men. This is a garrison of nearly 400. Just how much food they need to survive a siege can be estimated from an example in the fifteenth-century writing of Christine de Pisan. She listed the following provisions for a garrison of 600 men for six months:

60 tons of Paris wheat, one-third baked into biscuit, the rest to be ground into flour. 40 tons of beans, 2 tons of peas, 120 pipes of wine, 2 pipes of vinegar, 1 pipe [of] oil. 1 ton salt, 1 pipe [of] salted butter, 10–12 lbs. of rice, 50 lbs. of spices, ginger, pepper, etc., 15 lbs. of almonds, 2 lbs. of saffron, 2 quarters mustard seed. 100 oxen live or salted, 100–120 fletches bacon, 160 sheep. As much poultry "as men will", 1,000 eels [presumably smoked or dried], 25 barrels of herring.[13]

Fearing the approach of the English, French knights ride through villages near the castle burning homes, barns, crops, and orchards to deny food and shelter to the approaching English. Terrified villagers hurriedly gather what possessions they can and leave their burning homes, heading toward the castle in the hopes of finding sanctuary.

Often, food and water can be the most important ammunition a castle can have to withstand a siege. Any refuge is only as safe as its water supply, and often a shortage of food and water will cause a garrison to surrender long before the fortification walls are breached. A castle's water supply frequently offers a more vulnerable target than either its food supply or its walls. Although a reliable well, in or near the keep, is one of the basic necessities of any castle, wells sometimes run dry, and when a castle's well runs dry during a siege, the results can be disastrous.

With the castle supplied and secure, the French turn their attention to providing a properly frustrating welcome for the approaching English, who are now less than a week's march away.

Messengers are sent out from the four castles guarding the valley to announce to peasants in the district that they must leave their land immediately. Those who are not gone by the next day are driven out. When they are gone, any surviving crops, orchards, storehouses, and the remaining villages are burnt; anything that might offer food or shelter to the enemy must be destroyed. The French are determined that if they are going to be trapped in their castles, they will have any and all supplies they might need, and anything they cannot take into storage will be destroyed. The French have ruined the land around them and sealed themselves inside their castles, and just in time. The English army is within two days' march of the valley.

The Standoff

Our English army has been marching across Normandy hoping to meet the French in open battle, but as we have seen, detachments have been dispatched from the main army to besiege and reduce four castles guarding the valley pass. For the rest of the book, we will turn our attention away from the main army to one of the castles on the valley floor, its garrison, and the detachment sent to subdue it. We have established that the French garrison is well stocked, armed, and provisioned, and houses a contingent of 400 able men. The English have dispatched a force of 2,200 men to besiege and hopefully capture the fortress. The English are also well supplied and confident of at least two months in which to accomplish their task before having to face a French relief force.

As they cross the valley, the English are confronted by a large and formidable fortress, and their unit commander must decide the most logical way to bring it under his control. Committing to a siege is a serious undertaking, and only a fool would storm an undamaged fortress in broad daylight and seriously hope to overwhelm it. Although it is often said that some castles were never captured because they were impregnable, it is just as certain that some goals that cannot be accomplished by force can be achieved by the offer of generous terms, starvation, or treachery. Whenever possible, a garrison would be persuaded to surrender, or starved into submission. Sometimes, a traitor could be bribed to let the attackers in, by far the most cost-effective means of taking a castle. But diplomacy, the code of chivalry, and common sense dictate that after the English properly display their superior power, discipline, and determination, the French should be given an opportunity to surrender.

The English begin the negotiating ceremony as though they were hosting a tournament. The attackers line up their troops, column after column, wave after wave: scalers, miners, foot soldiers, engineers, archers, infantry, and cavalry. In full battle dress, with flags and banners flying, the commander

The English and the French face off, neither side willing to back down from the inevitability of a full-scale siege.

marches his entire column up to the main gate and deploys his forces to completely encircle the castle. The arrival of such an overwhelming display of force might persuade the garrison to capitulate at once, or after an honorable interval, whereupon they might be allowed to march away with all the "honors of war." The French, for their part, line the battlements, walls, and towers with every man in the garrison as a show of force and preparedness. The English do not yet know how many defenders they face, so the garrison plays up its strength as best they can. Suffice it to say that if the French refuse to deliver up their castle to the enemy, they face weeks or months of hunger, hardship, and dwindling numbers, which will perhaps end in brutal massacre. One thing is already clear: No one is going to get in or out of the fortress without tremendous effort unless they agree to terms.

The faceoff that results from this initial phase of intimidation should be familiar to any chess player. All of the pieces are in their starting ranks, and the players are staring each other down. Because both sides know the same limited range of military tactics, only by the cleverest and most subtle execution—and by pure tenacity—can one side hope to gain a real advantage over the other. But before the two sides can begin their "chess game" they need to agree on the terms, rules, and stakes. Thus we move into negotiations. After all of the preparations, talk, threats, posturing, and negotiations have occurred, the first pawn will be moved out of rank, and the bloody, dreaded siege will begin.

Chapter Five

THE OPENING GAMBIT

Negotiation, Threat, and Escalade

The English surround the fortress, deploying units to cut off any avenue of access or escape. Ideally, the strength of these units is evenly distributed, leaving no gap or weak point in the offensive line. When the code of chivalry has been properly honored, the commander of the besieging force calls upon the garrison to surrender before he commences hostilities. A herald is sent to the walls of the castle to announce that all supply lines and means of escape have been cut and the defenders are requested to surrender. This seemingly "civilized" bit of diplomacy is actually a matter of pure practicality. Mounting a siege places a tremendous economic burden on the attacking army. Sieges not only cost lives but time and money as well. Feudal troops may be required

Left: The English commander and his men are determined to subdue the castle.

Below: English knights, soldiers, archers, and men-at-arms array themselves in front of the castle walls to display their force in numbers to the French in the hopes of intimidating them into surrendering without a fight.

After making a proper show of their might, the English herald calls for the surrender of the castle. The French refuse.

meet in a pavilion erected in the open field between the opposing lines. In most cases, however, terms and proposals were carried between the encampments by heralds and intermediaries in what today might be referred to as shuttle diplomacy. By remaining behind their respective lines, the commanders not only ensure their personal safety, but also give themselves time to ponder the implications of the opposition's offer and to devise properly diplomatic—and often ambiguous—wording for a reply.

At the Siege of Breteuil, Jean de Froissart recorded the following negotiations, beginning with an offer from the besieging forces:

"Sirs, I have been sent to you by the Prince, who is willing to make you what I think is a very generous offer. He says that, if you will become his prisoners and surrender this fortress which is not defensible, he will spare your lives and give you the most honourable treatment."

"Sir John," replied Lord Boucicant, "very many thanks to the Prince for his generous offer, but we do not feel disposed to accept it. God forbid that he should capture us so easily."

"What, Lord Boucicant," said Sir John, "do you think yourself such splendid knights that you can hold this fortress against the Prince and his army, with no prospect of relief from any quarter?"

"Chandos, Chandos," replied Boucicant, "I don't consider myself a splendid knight, but we should be crazy to accept the kind of terms you are offering, and crazier still to give ourselves up when there is as yet no need for it. Please tell my lord the Prince to do

to stay in the field beyond the limits of their required service, and mercenaries demand regular payment. Consequently, any reasonable diplomatic means will be sought to avoid the necessity of an extended siege.

Castellans reticent to surrender their fortresses could sometimes be encouraged to see reason through negotiation, veiled threats, or outright intimidation. Occasionally, the reputation of an attacking commander was such that his mere appearance in the field could induce a stronghold to surrender, but such a commander would need to have a reputation as being either a brilliant tactician or notoriously brutal.[14]

Direct negotiations between opposing commanders certainly took place on some occasions. When they did, the leaders would

*The French comman-
der, above, and the
English commander,
right, exchange a series
of ambiguous letters
offering a negotiated
settlement. Privately,
each hopes that his
king will send reinforce-
ments to strengthen his
chances at winning an
all-out battle.*

*whatever he thinks best, and we will await
him here in all confidence."*

If the French at our siege choose to
accept terms of surrender, custom allows the
garrison to march out unharmed, often in possession of their arms, horses, and equipment;
after all, the objective of the siege is to capture
a castle, not to massacre inhabitants. However,
if the call to capitulate is rejected, the English
are completely within their right to sack the
castle and slaughter all its inhabitants. But, as
in all things diplomatic, the decision to fight or
surrender is never clear cut.

Because castles were held by a lord in
service to a superior lord, or directly answer-
able to the king, it was not uncommon for a
garrison commander to find himself in a
quandary when faced with a formidable enemy
and no clear instructions to follow. Should he
surrender immediately and save his men, or
hold out, risking his life and those of his men
should the castle fall? Thus, on occasion, a
castellan would formally request permission to
send to his lord for instructions during the
negotiations, or even during hostilities, in
order to ascertain his orders. Time limits were
often built into negotiations stipulating that
unless relieved by a given date, the castle would
surrender.

At this point, our own French castle
retains a significant advantage over the
besiegers. From the elevated position of their
battlements, the castellan and his knights can
survey the English force and gauge its
strength. The English, for their part, can only
make estimates as to the size of the French garrison, its supplies of ammunition, food, and
water.

The French, reluctant to relinquish their
king's land and fortress to the invaders, while
confident in their own ability and the strength
of their castle, refuse to surrender. Froissart
quotes one French castellan calling down from
the battlements of his castle, "You will not take
this land whilst one stone stands upon another." Despite this frustrating rebuttal, before
the English commander commits his forces to a
prolonged siege, he will test the strength and
resolve of the French garrison through an
escalade—an all out attempt to scale the walls
of the castle—in the hope of forcing the con-
frontation to a quick end. To signal the French
that negotiations are over and that battle will
commence, the English fire a single arrow into
the castle doors. This symbolic gesture was
often used by attackers to let the defenders
know that a siege had officially begun.

Although an escalade is one of the few
reliable ways to test the defenders' capabilities,
it is unlikely that any reasonably prepared castle will be taken in an initial assault. The tactic
is also a notorious meat grinder. The English
may lose anywhere from 10 to 25 percent of
their force in the attempt, but the siege is
young and the soldiers are eager, confident,
and enthusiastic. If an escalade is going to be
mounted at all, it needs to be done now, at the
beginning.

The surest way to test the strength of a
garrison and a castle's defenses in general is to
launch simultaneous assaults at a number of
points along the outer wall. By doing so, the
attentions—and the strength—of the defenders
are split. The English commander divides his
force into scaling parties and splits each of
these units into several smaller groups, which
will attack in four-hour shifts. This maneuver
takes advantage of the fact that any English soldier not directly engaged in an attack can move
to the safety of his own lines and relax. The
French, on the other hand, are trapped in their
fortress and must remain constantly vigilant if
they are to survive the assault. The English
commander hopes that the escalade will, over
the next twenty-four hours or so, reveal any

As the escalade begins, English archers provide cover fire for their comrades who have been charged with scaling the outermost set of walls.

One of many scaling parties reaches the base of the walls and erects its ladders.

As they begin their climb toward the top of the walls, the French are preparing to drive them back.

The first scalers are met with a hail of boiling water and quick-lime, which filters through their armor and boils their flesh and burns their eyes.

weak points in the defenses that he can exploit in the next phase of the operation.

At the forefront of the assault are the scalers who use ladders to mount the walls. Climbing a ladder may seem a simple enough task, but scaling ladders need to reach from ground to parapet, easily a distance of twenty to forty feet or more.

Scaling ladders were crude wooden affairs, sometimes fitted with iron hooks at one end to grip the edge of the wall, giving the climbers a firm hold as they tried to reach the top. Some ladders even had iron spikes at the base to dig into the ground to give firm footing. Those without spikes were secured with wedges to keep them from "kicking out" when they were mounted. Because the exact height of the wall could not be determined until the army was on site, scaling ladders could be built only after the two sides faced each other.

Other types of ladders were used on various occasions. The *Gesta Stephani* mentions ladders made of thongs (obviously rope ladders) used in the night attack that Robert Fitz Hubert made on Devizes in 1140. Several fifteenth-century treatises depict ladders made of straps and buckles, others which extended like hinged trellises, as well as heavy wheeled ladders that could be pushed against a castle's walls. Regardless of their design, the hastily constructed ladders sometimes broke under the combined weight of a half dozen heavily armored men.

Combine the fact that the climbers were in full armor, carrying weapons, and under attack with the fact that the wall guards were trying to topple their ladder, and the task of scaling a castle wall appears daunting, if not impossible. The art of using a scaling ladder was one of strength and speed: A good climber had to be able to hook his ladder over the wall and be half way to the top before the defenders on the wall could begin to dislodge it. Once the scaler reached the halfway point, the weight distribution made dislodging the ladder a supreme effort.

At our siege, while the English scalers race across the no-man's-land separating their lines from the castle, their comrades provide cover fire to drive the French back from the parapets. The hail of missiles is provided by ranks of archers, crossbowmen, and slingers firing from behind large wooden shields, known as pavises, which are positioned at a convenient distance from the castle. Protected by this artillery barrage, the scalers cross the killing field (as best they can, wearing full armor and hauling ladders). They scream their battle cries to drown out the shrieks of anguish from the wounded and dying littering the ground around them.

The first major obstacle they encounter as they cross the open field is the forward ditch. The ditch may have been filled with sharpened stakes, to slow the scalers' advance and make them easier targets, or sewn with caltrops—nasty four-pointed "stars" of sharpened iron that can pierce a man's shoe sole and foot to the bone.

If the ditch is a water-filled moat, a scaling party might employ portable wooden bridges, but these, too, have to be dragged across the open field. In most cases, the soldiers simply push forward through the ditch or swim across the moat. But as tenaciously as the English try to mount the walls, the French try to stop them. The wall guards frantically employ iron bars to dislodge the ladders from the tops of the walls. French bowmen and slingers fire at the oncoming English from the protection of parapets and arrow loops.

The fighting men and archers assembled themselves under their banners and began a fierce assault on the castle. The archers stood along the banks of the moat, shooting so

Left: While a wall guard is distracted, an English scaler makes it over the parapet, but the next man is not so lucky.

Right: A French soldier wielding a halberd forces him to choose between retreat or being hacked to death before he reaches the wall.

steadily that the defenders dared not show themselves on the battlements. Others launched on doors and hurdles with picks and mattocks.... Reaching the foot of the wall, they hacked and hammered away at it. Up above... the defenders hurled down stones and flints, and pots of quicklime, which inflicted terrible wounds on those they fell upon....

As we can see from Jean de Froissart's eyewitness report on the siege of Romorantin in 1356, defenders dropped an interesting variety of missiles on the attackers including, but by no means limited to, the following: sledges of rocks to knock the scalers off of their ladders; manure to get in the eyes of the assailants and

make their work additionally repulsive; red-hot iron pellets to insinuate themselves into gaps in armor; flaming bundles of straw to burn not only the scaling parties but their ladders as well; quicklime, which could filter through the visor of a helmet or through gaps in armor to burn away skin and eyes; sulfur to burn out the attackers' lungs; boiling pitch, which not only scalded flesh but also coated the ladders to make them both flammable and sticky.

Even without the hail of death from the battlements, scaling a ladder in full armor was exhausting and dangerous work. During the siege of Caen in 1346, English knight Sir Edmund Springhouse slipped off of his ladder and landed in the ditch below, breaking his leg. Before his comrades could pull him to safety, the French threw enough bundles of burning straw on him to roast him alive inside his armor.

To make the job of the scaling parties even more difficult, defenders constructed hoardings at strategic points along the curtain

Wooden hoardings projecting beyond the curtain walls make it difficult, if not impossible, for English scalers to reach the French guarding the parapets along some sections of the castle's walls.

the deck of the barge, making the task even more unsteady and precarious. "Weapons rained down on them like a hailstorm, stones, beams, jars of burning pitch and masses of iron." We are given a comprehensive account of the casualties:

Another as he dies, collapses in the middle of the boat on his dying comrade, and gives him his last embraces as they go down, comrade with comrade, to the infernal regions. Another is

wall. Primarily intended to overhang the parapet and command the base of the wall, these wooden shelters also deprive the scaling ladders of a resting place. A scaling party unfortunate enough to be sent against a hoarded wall will find themselves diverted onto the roof of the shelter and unable to reach the wall walk protected within. Scaling parties faced with hoardings usually attempted to burn them before scaling the wall, but even this can prove a difficult prospect because the wood in any recently constructed hoardings will be too green to burn.

Any of the English attackers lucky enough to reach the top of their ladder will likely be greeted by a Frenchman wielding a sword or axe. It is only through a combination of speed and sheer luck that an attacker has a chance to reach the parapets and fight on level ground.

Guillaume Le Breton gives us a graphic account of an assault during a siege. In this particular case, the attackers have crossed an extensive moat on assault barges to reach the base of the wall. He reports that in some places, the scaling ladders stand directly on

This diagram of the hoardings shows how defenders are provided with a maximum of protection from enemy fire, while still having a clear shot at those in the field beyond the castle as well as those at the base of the walls. The roof of the hoarding also denies scalers access to the parapet walls, even if they climb on top of the hoarding.

deprived of a foot, another of his eyes, another of his ears. One falls with gushing entrails, one with his throat cut, there a thigh is shattered with a staff, here brains are scattered with a club. One man's hand is shorn off with a sword, another forfeits both knees to an axe. And still no one draws back from the fight until the pitch poured from above causes them to step back. One groans as he breathes his last from a sword stroke in the face....

And so on. Grim though it may sound, this is a truer picture of medieval warfare than romantic legend conveys.

While the shower of arrows, bolts, stones, hot iron pellets, quicklime, boiling water, and pitch rains down from the walls, the English knights valiantly continue the attack. The fighting is hazardous, frightening, and almost certainly doomed to failure, and the English commander knows it. Only through sheer courage, tenacity, and a lot of luck can the English hope to gain even marginal ground during this initial escalade. Meanwhile, a group of their comrades test the strength of the castle's main door with a hand-held battering ram wielded under the protection of a makeshift canopy of shields known as an "iron turtle." Although it is doubtful that such a small ram can damage the great wooden door, if the door happens to be loose on its hinges or if the wood has been allowed to rot, there is a chance it might give way. As we discussed in chapter 2, the main gate is an even more dangerous line of approach than the curtain walls. Even if the English manage to get through the main door, the defenders will probably drop a portcullis behind them, trapping them in a murderous passage between the entrance and an inner gate.

It is unlikely that the small ramming party will break through the main gate, but their pur-
pose, like the scaling parties, is to gather intelligence. The intent of the initial escalade is to assess the strength of the fortress and its garrison. On the other hand, any knight or scaling party that actually manages to force a breach in the defenses will be lionized as heroes. There may not be another opportunity for personal heroism for months, so despite insurmountable odds, the English knights willingly dash themselves against the castle defenses.

After several successive waves of escalade fail to gain either a foothold on the walls or entry to the castle, the English commander recalls his forces. He assembles his officers to receive their reports and assessments on the defensive capabilities of the French. As a matter of policy and as a tactical ruse, the English will again call for the surrender of the garrison, threatening far worse punishment if the French insist on prolonging the inevitable English victory.

The French are also in consultation, gauging their own ability to withstand further assault, reassessing the supplies and provisions in store, and counting the casualties they have already suffered at the hands of the English who now surround their castle. They must weigh the odds of holding out until relief forces arrive against the agreed-upon deadline when the castellan will surrender. The French are uncertain of what, if any, weaknesses in their fortifications the English may have unveiled, but trusting that their castle and resolve are a match for any invader, they again refuse to surrender the fortress. The English now have little option except to dig in for a prolonged siege.

Just as the castle undertakes well-established defensive measures prior to attack, an army about to mount an extended siege also engages in standard operating procedures. As a part of their attempts to win the hearts and minds of the locals, the English set about fomenting dissension in the surrounding district through the spread of rumors. They attract as many dissidents and mercenaries as possible by luring them with the promise of plunder. Norman peasants recently driven out of their homes by the French make willing conscripts to fill the ditches and moats around the castle with dirt and straw to provide English soldiers and siege equipment with an easy approach to the walls.

To protect his position from soldiers on the castle wall, and from the possibility of a surprise attack by relief forces, the English commander orders defensive walls to be constructed around his encampment. The walls consist of a series of wide ditches that will slow down any approaching sorties from the castle or a surprise attack by relief forces. Dirt removed from the ditch will be piled on one side to create an earthwork embankment or rampart. Atop the rampart, to provide additional protection, a wooden breastwork resembling a low palisade fence will be constructed. One such wall will be erected between the camp and the castle, and another will separate the camp from the the main road to the castle—the most likely direction from which a French relief force would approach. Such a heavily fortified encampment is commonly referred to as a "siege castle" because an attacking force routinely builds a camp as large as the castle they are besieging. Siege castles may lack the massive fortification of their target, but many of them, particularly in instances of prolonged conflict, grew to dwarf nearby towns. Perhaps the most famous siege camp was the base of Edward III at the siege of Calais. Froissart writes:

As soon as the king of England arrived before Calais, he began in earnest to make full preparations for a regular siege. Between the town, the river and the bridge... he had houses built of heavy planks, thatched with

straw and brush-wood and set out in properly ordered streets, as though they were to be lived in for a dozen years. He was determined to stay there through winter and summer till Calais was his, without regard for the time and effort it might cost him. His new town had everything that an army could need and more, including a place to hold markets on Wednesdays and Saturdays. There were haberdashers and butchers' shops, stalls selling cloth and bread and all other necessities, so that almost anything could be bought there.... The King made no assaults on Calais, for he knew that the effort would be wasted. Desiring to spare his men and artillery, he said that he would starve the place out, however long it took, unless the King of France came to fight him again and raze the siege....

King Edward's siege castle at Calais was exceptionally grand. In most cases, they were usually rows of wooden hovels set behind the dirt palisades. The outline of one, a motte and bailey siege castle of 1174, survives about 400 yards from the gate of Huntingdon Castle in England. Several such temporary forts might be constructed during a siege so the invading army could effectively surround the target. In the current situation, however, there will be no time to build housing, and the English troops will have to make do with tents or live rough, sleeping on the ground.

Wherever possible, attackers take advantage of any terrain that might offer additional security or provide an advantage over the castle. On more than one occasion nearby church towers have been drafted into service. At Antioch, crusaders converted a local mosque into a siege castle and fortified its perimeter with tomb slabs. Geoffrey Talbot dug up the churchyard opposite Hereford Castle to make a rampart and placed siege engines on the bell tower. Any neighboring high ground, from which siege engines might launch artillery fire onto the defenders, was eagerly annexed to the besieger's position.

When English engineers select an appropriate site on which to position their siege engines, they begin to construct the cumbersome machines and the movable shel-

In conference after the first attack, the French assess their chances of holding out against the English in a prolonged siege.

ters that will be central to the next phase of the assault. Only the iron cogs, gears, lashing ropes, and intricate locking mechanisms of siege engines are taken on campaign—the massive support timbers and other wooden components will be foraged on site. Foraging parties fell any trees that remain in the area for construction material and fuel. Stones, rocks, and boulders of all sizes are gathered to provide ammunition for trebuchet, ballista, catapult, and slingers. While a search party is sent to locate a reliable water supply, tents are pitched, provisions stored, latrines dug, and everyone says their prayers.

Hundreds of English soldiers are engaged in constructing the defensive barricades and weaponry necessary to continue the siege. As they do so, they are constantly vulnerable to artillery fire from the walls of the castle. At the second siege of Le Puiset in 1112, the chronicler Suger remarks that the besiegers suffered greatly from the missiles of the garrison a stone's throw away, despite the fact that their work was shortened because the timbers used in constructing their compound had been prepared beforehand.

Cover for our English workers would be provided by archers and slingers who continually sweep the battlements with small arms fire. Despite the constant danger, this is a period of relative calm between the chaos of the escalade and the focused assault of the siege engines yet to come. At the moment, the contest is limited to English bowmen and slingers versus their French counterparts on the castle walls. As the lines are only a few hundred yards apart, combatants on both sides take advantage of the proximity and relative silence to amuse themselves and taunt their enemy by shouting the vilest insults that they can conjure up at their foes. We are all familiar with the childhood retort: Sticks and stones may break my bones, but names will never hurt me. Well, that, as we shall see, may not be specifically true.

Chapter Six

STICKS AND STONES

Small Arms Artillery

*Both sides attacked at once, blood-steeped weapons flew,
and men fell, cut down by them. Stones were loosed from
slings and arrows from bows. And the many wounds drove
out men's souls like leaves. The men inside threw down
hot lead and melted glass, striving to hurt by any means.
Those outside were protected by every kind of device:
shields, mantlets, battering rams, and unconquerable
siege-engines. As they come to the ditches, fighting
became fiercer, blood-drenched were the swords....*
—John of Garland describing the Siege of Toulouse
by Simon III of Montfort in 1218

As the English army constructs its encampment, volley after volley of stones, arrows, and crossbow bolts are exchanged by the opposing forces. Still, this is comparatively calm. The English are busy fortifying their position while the French recover from the initial escalade by tending to their wounded and repairing damaged hoardings. Soon both sides will raise the stakes in their bloody game by introducing siege engines to the playing field, but it will take days (or even weeks) to have them built, assembled, and moved into position. In the interim, English archers and slingers, positioned behind pavises and earthen ramparts, are primarily concerned with protecting their camp. During this period, the English are in as much of a defensive position as the French.

For their part, French artillerymen take advantage of the vulnerability of the enemy to reduce their numbers. Until the siege engines are complete, the contest remains one of small arms versus small arms, carried out at a range of 200 to 400 yards. This artillery, in the form of sling, crossbow, and longbow, remains fundamental to every phase of the assault and defense, so we will take advantage of this relatively calm period to focus on the contribution and effectiveness of these weapons.

CROSSBOWMEN

The French anticipated and planned for their current position. As previously discussed, most of the professional soldiers normally stationed at the castle were called to join the main body of the French army. This left a defensive force limited to the "household guard" (privately employed by the castellan), augmented by relatively untrained troops gathered from nearby towns and villages. With the majority of his 400-man garrison untrained and unaccustomed to the demands of martial exercise, the castellan's obvious choice was to equip his troops with crossbows.

Of ancient origin, the crossbow (or arbalest) rose to prominence in Europe in the twelfth century—its first recorded appearance in western warfare being the Battle of Hastings, 1066, when the Normans used both

the arbalest and the shortbow. The arbalest consisted of a short, powerfully sprung bow mounted on a straight wooden stock.[15] The thick bowstring was pulled back and held in the spanned (cocked) position by a latch or nut triggered by a lever under the stock. The bolt (arrow) was placed in a groove on top of the stock, in front of the bowstring. The archer raised the weapon to his cheek, took aim, and discharged the missile by raising the lever, which released the bowstring.

Early crossbows could (with some effort) be spanned by hand, but as bows grew more powerful and stiff, mechanical devices had to be employed to cock them. By the thirteenth century, spanning was done with the aid of a hook attached to the arbalester's waist belt. The bowman placed his foot in a stirrup fixed to the front of the weapon, stooped to catch the bowstring in the hook on his belt, then by using the

This drawing, based on an illumination in William of Tyre's manuscript written between 1250 and 1260, clearly shows crossbowmen assaulting a fortified tower. Note that the defender is retaliating by throwing rocks on his assailants.

whole force of his body to straighten himself, he could span the bow and catch the string on the retaining nut. Crossbows of the fifteenth century (of the type now in use by our French garrison) were spanned with the aid of a windlass (or "cranequin"), a small mechanical device incorporating a winding handle and ratchet. The cranequin wound the string into place with little expenditure of strength, but it was slow work.

Although vastly outclassed in speed by the longbow, the arbalest was a formidable weapon; efficient, accurate, and hard-hitting, with a range of up to 400 yards. Its advantage over the longbow was that its user needed neither strength nor training. Firing a crossbow took no special physical ability, and at moderate ranges, the flatter trajectory of the bolt was

easier to predict than the arc of an arrow. Its disadvantage was in the time it took to reload. Modern experiments have shown that three shots a minute is a good rate of fire when using a cranequin; four to six shots a minute are possible with a light crossbow spanned by muscle power or a belt hook. A practiced longbowman, on the other hand, could consistently achieve double that rate.

The arrow shot by the crossbow, called a bolt or quarrel, was shorter and stouter than a longbow shaft, with a heavier head, fletched with leather or thin wooden flights. These bolts inflicted such dreadful wounds that the Vatican's Lateran Council of 1139 prohibited the use of the "treacherous, murderous" crossbow amongst Christian nations, but allowed its use against infidels. Nevertheless, it was too

Though powerful enough to drop a charging horse at a hundred yards, and easy enough to operate that a novice could master it in a day, the crossbow had severe limitations. Slow to load and inaccurate at long range, crossbows proved ineffective in open field battle. In a siege, however, where anyone might be conscripted to guard a wall and parapets provided protection for reloading, it was an ideal weapon.

Safe within the recesses of the hoardings, crossbowmen, whether skilled professional soldiers or amateurs only a few hours on the job, presented a very real danger to enemy soldiers as they approached the castle.

Though the knights, secure in their heavy armour, had no scruples in riding down and killing the leather-clad foot-soldier, it is entertaining to read of the fierce outcry they made when the foot-soldier retaliated with steel cross-bow.... The knights called Heaven to witness that it was not honourable warfare to employ such weapons in battle, the fact being that they realized that armour was no longer the protection to their persons which it was before the days of heavy crossbows....

good a weapon to ignore, and despite the papal ban, it was widely used by Christian against Christian.

We know surprisingly little about the performance of medieval crossbows. Experiments in the nineteenth century suggest ranges equal or superior to the conventional bow; the inferior flight characteristics of a bolt compared to the conventional arrow might suggest that accuracy dropped off more quickly, but against this may be set the greater consistency of the arbalest's mechanical release. At shorter ranges, the bolt had tremendous impact and penetration, smashing through plate armor with ease. In his seminal work on the subject, straightforwardly entitled *The Crossbow*, Sir Ralph Payne-Gallwey writes:

The crossbow enjoyed preferential status over other bows throughout continental Europe. It was a favorite hunting weapon in Germany, Switzerland, and northern Italy. Regular practice was encouraged by competitions and regulations. Towns and villages formed shooting clubs, and members paraded proudly with their bows and guild banners. (Some of these clubs still exist today.) Some districts became famous for their crossbowmen and mercenaried their companies to other cities: The Genoese fought for the French at Crécy (see chapter 3), and we read that the men of Guyenne were "courageous, light headed and good men-at-arms, the common people are all crossbowmen." Swiss and German armies of the fifteenth century frequently fielded mixed companies of crossbowmen and hand gunners as skirmishers. Crossbowmen mostly fought on foot; but the introduction of the cranequin, or rack, made reloading on horseback possible.

Richard I of England (reigning from 1189–1199) employed crossbowmen in his army when fighting French King Philip Augustus (1180–1223) and his well-organized bodies of foot and mounted arbalesters. These regiments became so important that their commander was given the title of Grand Master of Crossbowmen, a high post in the French army. (It was not until 1515 that the office was united with that of Grand Master of Artillery.) Edward I of England (1272–1307) hired expensive Gascon arbalesters for his early Welsh campaigns, until he became enamored with the virtues of the cheap, fast-shooting Welsh longbow. In 1282 Edward fielded 850 crossbowmen, by 1289 this had fallen to 105, and in 1292 a mere 70 were fielded. On the continent, however, the crossbow remained a popular weapon throughout the fourteenth and fifteenth centuries.

The crossbow quarrels fell like rain, the clouds were thick with dust... the... infantry, knife in hand, crawled under the bellies of the horses and disemboweled them... (Florentine Chronicle)

In open battle, the arbalester often used a heavy stationary shield (or pavise) to provide cover while he spanned his weapon, but the crossbow was most effective when used in the defense of a castle or walled city under siege; the crenellated fortress walls providing cover to cock and reload the weapon. Often, the rate of fire at a single loophole would be doubled by stationing two arbalesters at the same post, one shooting while the other reloaded.

Back at our seige, the commander of the English force, concerned that crossbow bolts are flying from the castle walls at a range of up to 400 yards, has ordered his own artillerymen to return fire so as to busy the defenders. Ramparts must be dug in the killing ground separating the two opposing forces. The English artillerymen have to keep the diggers

alive long enough to complete their task, lest they find themselves with a shovel in their hands. To mitigate their vulnerability, the English move portable defenses into place.

shields and pavises

Shields were no longer in standard use among knights of the fifteenth century, the development of full armor providing the wearer sufficient protection. Exceptions were the round, oval, or kidney-shaped shields still favored by some Italian and Spanish troops, who retained a light cavalry tradition; the bucklers of the infantry; and the much larger freestanding pavises which protected artillerymen during a siege.

Up to two yards high, slightly curved, and immensely strong, pavises (or mantlets) were usually made of wood covered with hide and painted in heraldic colors to identify their owner. Pavises could either be highly decorated objects, designed as much for display as for combat, or they could be very businesslike defenses. Larger pavises often had triangular holes cut at eye level for vision and shooting, and some had hooks and rings attached to their edges so they could be linked in rows. Nearly all were fitted with either supporting props and/or ground spikes on the bottom edge so they could be propped upright in the field.

The use of small-arms artillery was fundamental during all phases of the siege. In reference to the effectiveness of artillery during an escalade, Jean de Froissart records:

Early the next morning all of the English fighting men armed themselves, including the archers. They assembled under their banners and began a fierce assault on the castle. The

Shooting volley after volley from behind large shields, known as pavises, the English rain arrows on the French so thick and fast that they hardly dare show their heads above the battlements.

archers stood behind their breast works by the banks of the moat, shooting so steadily that the defenders hardly dared to show themselves on the battlements. At this, the English archers took one pace forward and poured out their arrows so thickly and evenly that they fell like snow on the heads of their enemies....

In the case of our own siege, the English artillerymen are certainly subjected to a more spartan existence than the French. The French, when not engaged in action, can withdraw into the heart of the fortress where they are (at least for the time being) safe from enemy threat. Supplies in the fortress are carefully rationed out, but they sleep in a warm, dry place until, renewed and invigorated, they can return to their posts and their assault on the enemy. English artillerymen, on the other hand, sleep under wagons or bushes or with their backs against any large stone, which may

have absorbed some warmth from the sun and might help protect them from the rain. Barracks are sometimes built to shelter common soldiers, but only when an army undertakes a siege of many months' duration. The English artillerymen could have sheltered in the barns that served the castle farms if the French had not burned them all. Perhaps some of the knights and officers will share their tents or pavilions with the artillerymen, but whatever the case, shelter for archers and slingers is hardly a paramount concern of the English commander at this point.

SLINGERS

The heaviest artillery barrage the English can direct toward the enemy comes from massed numbers of peasants armed with slings. The sling, like so many weapons in the medieval arsenal, was in common use in

Biblical times. Ever since David slew Goliath more than three thousand years earlier, the lower classes have practiced using slings as a cheap and effective weapon against small game, marauding wolves, and human enemies alike. Today, the slingers skills may help level the playing field. Hurling stones may seem a crude and unsophisticated method of attack for the proud armies of the fourteenth and fifteenth centuries, but military commanders saw a great advantage in using ranks of slingers. The small stones and pebbles that make up their ammunition are free and plentiful, aiming the weapon requires no special training, and the assault can be kept up as long as the slinger's arm holds out. Although the sling possesses neither the deadly force nor the range of the bow, the hail of whizzing stones can force a defender to keep his head behind the safety of the parapets—effectively eliminating him as a threat.

When imagining the events of the siege, modern historians often overlook the fact that medieval battles raged on in relative silence. Because the siege lacks the noise of gun fire, jet engines, or exploding artillery, both sides are able to amuse themselves, and anger the enemy, by screaming profanities and taunting each other. As far as we know, specific records of these taunts do not survive, but we can be certain that they included colorful epithets concerning the enemies' mothers, wives, and sweethearts. It is difficult to know for whose benefit the insults were hurled, because there would inevitably have been language barriers. A soldier probably shouted profanities as much to amuse his comrades as to anger the enemy. One thing is certain, however, the sheer frustration of being pinned down by jeering peasants hurling stones and insults, was often enough to cause a man to react without thinking, a fatal miscalculation that could expose him to the deadly assault of the longbow.

LONGBOWMEN

Introduced into the English ranks in the early thirteenth century by the Welsh, the longbow was the most devastating weapon on the medieval battlefield. Longbowmen made up a considerable part of the English army. Although only 700 of the 2,200 Englishmen at our siege are archers, they make up over half of the main army. The English tactic of using massed archers in the thousands proved most effective at Crécy, Poitiers, and Agincourt. But, as we have discussed, this tactic is really only applicable to open field engagements.

Here, at the siege, artillery is necessary to provide cover for other forms of assault, but the besiegers do not require archers in the thousands as does their main army making its way into the heart of Normandy. At the siege, only about one-fourth of the besieging force are archers and that, in itself, speaks to their effectiveness.

Their effectiveness, however, earns neither the weapon nor the bowman the respect of the haughty noblemen in armor. The code of chivalry demands that knights engage their enemies in "honorable" face-to-face combat with sword and lance; bowmen, on the other hand, kill from a safe distance. Killing in such a manner is considered cowardly and unchivalrous. Consequently, archers are despised partly for their lack of chivalry but also because they are more effective on the field than the mounted nobility. Though this problem faces artillerymen of all sorts, at the time of our seige, the incontrovertible victories at Crécy and Agincourt are slowly beginning to influence the nobility's perception of archers.

The English archer of the Hundred Years' War was a true professional fighting man, who took great care of his weapons and cropped his hair short so that it would not blow in his eyes to disturb his aim. Most archers must have been big, fit men. The secret of their power was lifelong practice. Successive kings of England ordered that all able-bodied men should practice regularly: Edward IV issued statutes in 1466 ordering that every Englishman and Irishman between the ages of sixteen and sixty should have "an English bow of his own length." As a result of such preparation, in 1474 King Edward had 14,000 well-trained archers under his command.

An archer marched into battle with a sheaf of twenty-four or thirty-six arrows tied in a bundle at his belt. He carried his bow unstrung in a case, his bowstrings and beeswax in a pouch at his hip. In action he stood in a stately position, his arrows stuck in the ground beside him, ready for rapid use; when these were gone, one of the young lads who attended the army's baggage brought another sheaf from the arrow wagon.

During the fourteenth and fifteenth centuries, the English archer's pay changed little. While in service "out of England," it was six pence per day for a mounted archer, three pence for a foot archer; for garrison service within England, it was respectively four pence and three pence. Many contracts specified that if pay fell in arrears by more than three or six months, the contract was null. Bonuses were also frequently paid. Thus a mounted archer earned at least three times the pay of a skilled civilian worker, a foot archer one and a half times. Despite being despised by the chivalry, they were obviously a valuable asset.

Unlike a crossbowman, a skilled longbowman could not be created overnight. Mastery of the longbow depended, not on the strength of arm alone, but of the whole body. Its exponents were trained from youth, taught to lay their bodies to the bow, progressing through weapons of increasing size as they grew bigger and stronger. Medieval Englishmen were aware

of the training required and emphasized the importance of starting young (boys traditionally began training at age seven), growing up with the bow. Bishop Latimer's sermon to the young Edward VI in 1549 illustrates this:

In my time my poor father was diligent to teach me to shoot as to learn any other thing, and so I think other men did teach their children. He taught me how to draw, how to lay my body in the bow and not to draw with the strength of my arms as other nations do, but with the strength of my body. I had bows brought to me according to my age and strength and as I increase in them so my bows were made bigger, for men shall never shoot well except they be brought up in it.

A well-trained archer could be most daunting—even to a well-armored knight. As early as the twelfth century, Geraldus Cambrensis observed that "a soldier had his hip, which was sheathed in armor on both sides, penetrated by an arrow quite to the saddle, and on turning his horse round, received a similar wound in the opposite hip, which fixed him fast to both sides of his seat." A full-size longbow, some six feet in length, required a pull from 80 pounds to over 150 pounds draw weight. Plus the archer had to be capable of sustained shooting for several minutes at a time.

The requirements of archery in medieval warfare were completely different than those of the modern recreational archer; consequently marked differences in stance and technique exist (see sidebar on page 84). For the English archers, great emphasis was put on "strong shooting" and long range (Henry VIII made practice at long range compulsory), which meant using powerful bows. As previously mentioned, the ability to shoot such bows is not something easily achieved.

There was a difference in status between

archers recruited in wartime and those permanently retained by the nobility. A good retained archer was looked after well. We read in household accounts of expensive bows, arrows, and other equipment provided for them. In 1467 Daniel, one of Sir John Howard's household archers, received an annuity of £10 (compare this to the mounted archer's home service rate of £6.08, above), two gowns, a house for his wife, other clothes, and sums of money including 20 pence to attend a shooting match. In 1481 Sir John also gave Harry Mainwaring and Thomas Cooke sallets, brigantines covered with purple velvet, mail collars, "jacket and gusset," simple arm armor, and sheafs of arrows.

This list of accessories leads us to examine the equipment of the English archer of the fifteenth century. Although it may not seem directly connected with the siege, we should remember that archers comprised the bulk of both armies and were emerging as the dominant force on the battlefield. An examination of the archer's equipment may give us some understanding of this ongoing shift in military demographics.

As regards protective clothing, the archer augmented his clothing with whatever he could take from the enemy's dead or prisoners, including various pieces of armor and helmets. A popular item of bowman's apparel was the brigadine jacket, a sleeveless leather tunic lined with iron plates which allowed free movement of the arms. Monstrelet, in his chronicles, describes the English bowmen at Agincourt (1415) as being for the most part without armor and in jackets, without hats or caps, and often barefooted (to give surer purchase on the ground). An axe or sword usually hung at their girdles. St. Remy says many wore caps of *cuir bouilli* (boiled leather) and others of wicker work crossed over with bars of iron. An eyewitness description in 1483 from Dominic Mancini, a disinterested foreign observer, states:

> There is hardly any without a helmet and none without bows and arrows: their bows and arrows are thicker and longer than those used by other nations, just as their bodies are stronger than other people's, for they seem to have hands and arms of iron. The range of their bows is no less than that of our arbalests; there hangs by the side of each a sword no less long than ours, but heavy and thick as well. The sword is always accompanied by an iron shield [buckler].... They do not wear any metal armor on their breast... the common soldiery have more comfortable tunics that reach down below the loins and are stuffed with tow or some other soft material....

Commynes described Burgundian archers before the battle of Montlhery as follows: "We found all of the archers with their boots off and with a stake driven into the ground before them, and there were many barrels of wine broached for them to drink. From the small amount which I saw I have never seen men more willing to fight."

The Longbow

It is unlikely that the medieval archer would have called his weapon a longbow. The earliest references to the word are from the fifteenth century and were used in listings of equipment to differentiate longbows from crossbows; on their own they were simply called "bowes." It was not until the sixteenth century that the "longbow" (written either as one word or two) became common and was identified with a particular type of weapon. Whether the military adopted a bow already in common usage in civilian England or vice versa is a matter for argument, but this bow became so widespread in English society that it became known in Europe as the "English bow."

As the English army changed from one raised by feudal obligation to one of indentured or paid service, operating under central government control, the office of the ordinance became increasingly responsible for supplying equipment. The contemporary title for the longbow then was the "livery bow" as the issuing of weapons to the soldiers by the ordnance office was simply seen as an extension of that system. Then, as today, much of that equipment was made to prescribed government specifications.

The longbow has become so entrenched in history (and legend) as *the* medieval weapon that we often overlook the fact that it did not represent the only design of the bow in use in medieval Europe. Retained and levied archers brought their own bows of various types and sizes with them when they enlisted, but they would be reequipped with standard ordinance by the army. The longbow was chosen for military service because, although it was not technically the most efficient bow of the period, it was the most suitable. It was a well-made, relatively cheap, robust weapon that could be mass produced and was capable of projecting man-stopping missiles over a great distance at a fast rate of fire—the exact same criteria laid down for every infantry weapon up to the present day. The great advantage the longbow enjoyed over the crossbow was its rapid shooting: six or more arrows could be discharged in the time it took a crossbowman to shoot one bolt. A well-trained bowman could launch twelve arrows per minute over a range of up to 400 yards. A medieval observer stated: "A first-rate English archer who in a single minute was unable to draw and discharge his bow twelve times, with a range of 250 yards, and who in these twelve shots once missed a man, was very lightly esteemed." At closer range, and with more

time taken to aim, the longbow could be even more deadly.

The longbow was what is today called a "self-bow," (that is, a bow made from a single piece of wood). They were generally about six feet long and either straight or with a slight forward curve (of the sort known today as a reflexed bow). Bowyers, the makers of bowstaves, became privileged craftsmen, as did fletchers, who feathered the arrows. Since prehistoric times, yew has been considered the wood most suited for bow making, though other timbers such as elm, ash, and beech were also employed to prevent the total destruction of yew trees. The bowyer fashioned the six-foot shaft of rough wood into a delicate curve tapering outward from a two-inch diameter at the center and narrowing gradually to neat ends fitted with horn tips. The tips were notched to secure the bowstring of hemp or flax, which was regularly rubbed with beeswax to prevent fraying. Finished bows were supplied as "painted" or "white," that is, with or without a waxed or polished finish respectively.

Bow production was a well-established industry. Staves came from carefully tended plantations of pollarded trees. Royal statutes controlled and encouraged the trade. Edward IV's statute of 1472 is typical. Every vessel sailing for England from "any other city, town or country from whence any such bowstaves have been before this time brought" must bring in four bowstaves for each ton of merchandise. The numbers were carefully checked and the imports marked for quality: The staves—not yet shaped into finished bows—were to be "three fingers thick and squared, seven feet long, to be well got up, polished and without knots."

By royal order of 1475, a skilled bowyer should take about one and three-quarter hours to turn a stave into a bow costing no more than 3 shillings 4 pence. These were "livery" bows

The most noticeable difference between the present-day archer and his ancestor is in the aiming method, reflected by the point to which the arrow is drawn back. There are four basic methods of aiming, which can be categorized as follows: purely instinctive, semi-instinctive, point-of-aim (POA), and using a bow-sight or mark on the bow.

Purely instinctive is how we throw stones and darts. The brain receives information from the eye, makes all the necessary calculations about weight and distance, and passes this data to the arm. To be truly instinctive in archery, the actual mechanics of shooting should be an almost unconscious act, with all concentration centered on the eye—rather like changing gear when driving a car. Semi-instinctive is similar to the instinctive method above, but it also requires seeing the tip of the arrow in the periphery of vision and using it as a reference point.

Arrows, unlike bullets, only fly in a straight line for very short distances and, like artillery shells, travel in a parabolic curve. The POA archer establishes a point-blank range; that is, the distance at which, when sighting on the tip of the arrow, it flies to exactly where his eye is looking. For shorter and longer distances, the aim is not at the target but at a point below or above it. Use of

Proper use of the longbow demanded that the archer put the entire weight, and strength, of his body into his weapon.

a sight or mark on the bow is self-explanatory, but there is little evidence for their use in the medieval period.

Modern archers draw their arrows back to an "anchor" point on their face or chin, under the aiming eye. It is considered important to have this fixed reference point to ensure consistency of aim. Although there are many medieval illustrations depicting archers shooting with such a style, these are practically all of non-English origin. It is arguable that what distinguished the best English military archers from their European contemporaries was their ability to shoot powerfully and accurately at both long and short distances by drawing to the ear and aiming instinctively. Actually, the phrase "to the ear" is a generalization and might refer to any point between the ear and the breast (the latter being a natural "locking" point for the shoulder). To lower the drawing hand is, in effect, to raise the bow hand, but it is a difficult technique with heavy bows.

Although it counted among the deadliest of weapons on the medieval battlefield, mastery of the longbow required years of vigilant training.

It is commonly assumed that "drawing to the ear" means shooting a very long arrow—up to 36 inches according to some writers—on the premise that modern archers only have a draw length of 28 to 30 inches. This assumption overlooks the practicalities of the method and the restrictions imposed by wearing defensive apparel. If a right-handed archer stands as a modern archer does and simply extends his draw from chin to ear, the off-center line of the arrow makes it fly to the left. This angle is increased farther if the archer is wearing a helmet, for then it is necessary for the drawing hand to be farther away from the side of the head. To shoot straight, the archer has to bring his bow arm around to be in line with his drawing hand; this immediately shortens the draw length.

Another difference is in the position of the lead foot (nearest the point of the arrow). Modern archers stand sideways-on with both feet at ninety degrees to the target. Medieval illustrations show the leading foot pointed toward the target. The effect of this stance is to bring the shoulder round and "squarer-on" to the target, thereby increasing the clearance of the string path from the chest, especially important if the archer is wearing padded clothing or a breastplate. It also contributes to the reduction in draw length.

While a three-finger draw was certainly used (though usually by the genteel class), the great majority of medieval illustrations depicting professional archers show a two-finger hold. This would impart a sharper release because there would be less friction on the string when loosed; its use, however, was determined by the strength of the archer. The Englishman's two-finger "salute"—still used today as a defiant gesture—had its origins in the two-finger hold. The gesture was adopted by archers because the French threatened to cut off the drawing fingers of any archer they captured. (See The Battle of Agincourt in chapter 3.)

At a firing rate of ten to twelve arrows a minute, the longbow-man is more than a match for an enemy.

London and elsewhere as many armourers, fletchers, smiths and other artificers and workmen as are required for the making of armour, bows, bowstrings, arrows, arrowheads... and put them to work at the King's wages." Along with armorers and other craftsmen, bowyers accompanied the army on the march, though surprisingly for such a skilled job, they were paid only at the same rate as the foot archers. In time of war, a small army of fletchers, bowyers, and smiths would turn out bows and arrows by the ton; once again we are reminded that organization on this scale cannot have been simple or "primitive."

In the relative silence of battles fought with slings, arrows, and siege engines, soldiers punctuated their assaults on the enemy by screaming insults and making obscene gestures.

ARROWS

Many people have heard of the famous cloth yard arrow. Unfortunately the term is a literary invention. The description is a misquotation from a ballad of around 1465, spread into literature by seventeenth-century balladeers and poets. There is no historical justification for it, and much erroneous research has been done into the length of the cloth yard in order to establish a length for the war arrow.

War arrows were known as either livery, sheaf, or standard: livery because they were issued; sheaf from the Anglo-Saxon word for a bundle, or perhaps because twenty-four arrows bound together resembled a sheaf of grain; standard either because they were made to the

(army issue); the personal bow of a household archer might cost double that. During times of military preparation, the government not only bought up all the available stocks of bows and bowstaves, but also conscripted bowyers into full-time service. For example, in 1359 one William de Rothwell was ordered to "take in

length of the legal standard yard or, more probably, because the whole design was subject to government specification. War arrows had a large-diameter shaft so they could carry a large head to do maximum damage. To keep their weight to a minimum, the arrows were made of lightweight timber from many kinds of woods, in particular yew, Brazil, birch, elm, and aspen. The arrows, which were three feet long, were fitted with steel "piles" or points of various shapes and sizes, each designed for a specific purpose. The narrow bodkin head, for example, was used for penetrating armor; the crescent-shaped head was used to hamstring horses or to sever ship rigging; smaller lighter heads were used for longer distance arrows, and so forth. The fletcher (from the French *fléche*, meaning arrow) fitted each shaft with three feathers, goose feathers being the favored choice though swan, duck, and peacock fletchings were also used.[16]

There are references to different types of arrows—long-range "flight" arrows and heavier types—with different lengths of fletchings. An archer probably had his own favorite arrows, more expensive than "army issue." He was expected to arrive for service with a sheaf of twenty-four or thirty and might go into action with two sheaves, giving him ammunition for four to five minutes shooting. It is clear that immense reserves were necessary, and contemporary documents describe them in detail. In 1359, for instance, 20,000 bows, 850,000 arrows, and 50,000 bowstrings were gathered at the Tower of London. A 1475 supply list mentions 10,060 "sheffes"—more than a quarter of a million arrows.

These arrows were carried in chests or barrels in the wagons of the army's baggage train. A few contemporary illustrations show boxes of arrows without heads next to barrels of heads. Heads may have been jammed on prior to use or quickly set in place with wax.

The advantage of this would be the ease with which an arrow could be recovered from the spot where it had embedded itself, whether in the ground or a man's body, fitted with a new head, and reused. Furthermore, without their own supply of arrowheads, an enemy would be unable to shoot the arrow back.

PERFORMANCE

We should ask ourselves what kind of performance these bows could achieve. Simply put, the range of the bow depends on its power and the strength of the archer. Modern archers have shot bows with draw weights of 120 to 160 pounds, and no doubt the best of the highly trained medieval bowmen would have been capable of more. In the sixteenth century, Sir John Smythe wrote that war arrows should travel 240 yards, and "then some number of archers being chosen, that could with flights [lighter, long-range arrows] shoot 24 or 20 scores [480 or 400 yards], as there be many that can." Shakespeare speaks of 290 yards as a good shot; and a list of seventeenth-century archery practice grounds gives lengths up to 380 yards.

Numbers and speed were far more important in battle than mere range, however. Expert Burgundian writers of the day, who had witnessed the English in action, used their prowess as a figure of speech, speaking of shots flying "thicker than arrows in an English battle," and stating, "I am of the opinion that the most important thing in the world in battle is archers, but they must be in thousands, for in small numbers they do not prevail." Ten arrows loosed in a minute was a steady rate of shooting.[17] It was this barrage shooting which made the English truly deadly; a thousand archers could pour a hail of 10,000 to 12,000 shafts down on their foe every minute—and that Hainault and the Somme each supplied about 1,000 foot archers to the Duke of Burgundy's army.

By the end of the fifteenth century, the status and reputation of the archer was such that they were chosen for royal and noble guards. In the 1450s Charles VII of France had a Scottish archer guard, and in the 1470s, more than a thousand English bowmen served Charles the Bold of France, forming part of his *garde du corps*. A Burgundian captain wrote: "The English have been more watched and admired in our army and better esteemed than were our robes of cloth of gold and costly ornaments."

For all of his effectiveness, however, the glory days of the inimitable English archer were short-lived. A splendid weapon though it was in speed, accuracy, and economy, the

The craft of making good arrows was essential to the continued success of the English war effort. Shafts had to be cured to remain straight, tens of thousands of arrow heads had to be forged by blacksmiths, and 'fletches' made from goose quills had to be cut and carefully sewn onto each shaft.

Outraged that their English enemy would be so unchivalric as to allow peasant archers to draw on knights in open battle, the French swear to cut off the first two fingers of any archer they capture. Defiantly, the English archers taunt the enemy by displaying their fully operational fingers.

field armies typically had several thousand archers. By extension of this argument, at our siege, during times of concentrated assault such as an escalade, the English force of 700 archers can conceivably launch 7,000 to 8,400 arrows per minute into the fortress—presuming, of course, that their supplies hold out.

There were many excellent archers serving in continental armies, but their performance has been virtually eclipsed from memory by the dazzling performance of the English bowmen. The French raised companies of bowmen, and though it is not well-known, many Frenchmen were recruited into English archer companies in France. Flemish archers were frequently mixed with crossbowmen. A muster roll of 1476 notes

Arrows were made from more than a dozen different woods, but aspen was preferred, with ash a close second. The shape of the arrow varied, affecting its performance: parallel-sided, tapered (from the head backward), barreled (swelling out in the middle), or chested (with the swell set back towards the nock). The latter were the most aerodynamically efficient and were preferred by strong shooters; most arrows found in the wreck of the sixteenth-century *Mary Rose* were tapered. The sheer brute bulk of a medieval war arrow has to be seen to be appreciated.

The feathered flights, usually goose, were six to eight inches long; they were glued and often tied on with a spiral of fine thread. In the 1470s six wing feathers from every goose in the country were to be collected throughout the counties and towns of England and sent to London.

Arrow points came in a staggering variety of sizes and shapes, each with its own specific purpose. Short points were intended for firing at the rank and file of the enemy. Long, slender 'bodkin' points were used for piercing plate armor as well as the man inside of it; and wide crescent-shaped points for slashing the hamstrings and bellies of charging horses.

The points varied, but the narrow, square-sectioned bodkin was ideal for punching through mail and fabric armor. Plate armour stopped most arrows even at a fairly close range; the angle of impact was vital, but even an arrow striking at ninety degrees would rarely pierce the steel deep enough to wound seriously. Wounds to less well-protected bodies could be many inches deep, doing fatal internal damage (we should recall that Tudor archers recorded shooting arrows clean through an inch of seasoned timber).

longbow had the singular disadvantage of requiring practiced skill to handle effectively, "for men shall never shoot well unless they be brought up to it." This constant demand for expertise led to its eventual abandonment in favor of the handgun and long pike, both of which demanded vast organization, but little training.[18] In 1577, a century after the heyday of medieval English artillery, William Harrison lamented: "The French... turn up their tails and cry 'shoot, English!'... But if some of our Englishmen now lived that served King Edward the third, the breech of such a varlet should have been nailed to his bum, and another feathered in his bowels, before he should have turned about to see who shot the first."

Chapter Seven

RAISING THE STAKES

Siege Engines

For more than a week, archers and slingers have been wearing away at each other's nerves and each side's manpower with volley after volley of stones, bolts, and arrows. English scaling parties have repeatedly attempted to mount the castle walls and have just as repeatedly been driven back at a cost of over a hundred dead and many more wounded. While the English have been busy fortifying their position, both sides have been preparing to increase the level of violence and slaughter in the hope of forcing the siege to an early end. Soon, the English commander will set sappers and miners to work attacking the castle's foundations, but first, the strength of its walls (and the resolve of the French) will be tested under the brutal punishment of siege engines.

There were also frequent skirmishes near the gates and moat... which always took their toll in killed and wounded. Sometimes one side would come off best, sometimes the other, as is usual in this type of fighting. The English commander and his council now devised various means of attack to wear down the garrison through the construction of machines to harass the besieged. The besiegers set up great engines to hurl missiles by night and day onto the roofs and towers, which did much damage... (Froissart, *Chronicles*)

Having had ample time to prepare for the attack, the French will try to prevent the English from completing their siege engines before they wreak destruction on the fortress. For their part, the English are frantically assembling every size and type of war machine available so they can crush the French and rejoin the main body of their army as soon as possible.

Luck, and the greatest chance of winning the siege, was always on the side that had the largest number and variety of siege engines. The early advantage usually lay with the besieged because they could build their engines in peace time and store them in the castle grounds until such time as they were needed. The besiegers, on the other hand, had to transport dozens of wagon loads of cumbersome parts over long distances or trust that there would be adequate materials to construct the machines on-site when necessary.

Full-scale siege engines were so ponderous that moving them any significant distance was virtually impossible. For this reason, unless they could be transported by ship, the main mechanical components (winches, windlasses, and cordage, etc.) were hauled by cart to the site of the siege, while a frame was constructed with whatever timber survived in the neighborhood.

At our siege, to find enough timber of suitable size, the English engineers[19] and their work parties have to travel miles from their base camp. When enough trees of sufficient size are located, they still must be felled, cut, and shaped. After the massive timbers are dragged back to camp by animal or manpower, they must be shaped and fitted into a framework stable enough to withstand the recoil of a firing siege engine.

Engineers, carpenters, and laborers are scattered in small work parties at various locations near their camp and in the surrounding fields. The English are now at their most vulnerable, and they will remain constantly exposed to danger until the engines are completed.

In the *Gesta Francorum* (1099), Raymond of Augilers describes the making of siege engines for the assault on Jerusalem:

The duke and the counts of Normandy and Flanders placed Gaston of Béam in charge of the workmen who were constructing the siege-engines and were making fascines and earthworks for invading the walls. In the same way, Count Raymond placed William Embriaco in charge of his workmen on Mount Zion and the Bishop of Albara in charge of the Saracens and others who were bringing wood. The Count's men were making the saracens work like their slaves. Fifty or sixty of them carried on their necks a huge beam, which four pairs of oxen could not bear.

What can I say? Everyone united to further the task, by labor, by construction and by generally helping. No one was lazy and no one slacked. Everyone worked voluntarily, except for the craftsmen, who were paid from a collection taken among the people. But Count Raymond paid his workmen from his own coffers.

The French garrison began assembling their engines weeks ago when they first anticipated the English approach. Now, while the English prepare their engines, the French will lob a few short-range decoy shots out of the castle in the hope of convincing the English that their weapons have a far more restricted firing range than they actually do. If the English fall for the ruse, they may be foolish enough to set up their engines within reach of the French artillery, and the French might be able to destroy some of them before they are ever brought to bear on the castle. In games of this sort, timing is of the essence. Because the French possess a limited supply of ammunition, they must gauge their shots carefully and wait until the English engines near completion before they expose the full capabilities of their own weapons. Once the English begin the bombardment, the French may be able to augment their ammunition supply by launching incoming projectiles back at the attackers, or even by tearing masonry blocks from the walls of buildings in the castle yard. But, their hope is to preempt an assault barrage altogether by knocking out the English engines just before they reach completion.

The great variety of siege engines created by ancient and medieval engineers can only be categorized in one of two ways: by the type of object they threw ("petrarae" threw stones and "balistrae" launched arrows or javelins) or by their method of propulsion (tension, torsion, or counterweight). So many names have been so carelessly applied to these devices by medieval chroniclers, as well as later writers, it is often impossible to tell what kind of engine an author is actually talking about. The following names were commonly, and often indiscriminately, applied to siege weapons: "Balista," "Beugle," "Bible," "Bricolle," "Calabra," "Catapulta," "Engin," "Engin á verge," "Espringale," "Fronda," "Fundibulum," "Malvoisin,"

"Manganum," "Mangon," "Mangonel," "Martinet," "Matafunda," "Mate-griffon," "Petrary," "Perrier," "Robinet," "Scorpion," "Springald," "Tormentum," "Trebuchet," "Tripantum," "Wyvernier," and doubtlessly many more. This love of nicknames suggests that such machines were not abundant; conversely, the lack of mechanical description suggests they were so common that they aroused almost no excitement. So many names could also suggest that an almost endless variety of siege engines, but this was not the case.

Since many ancient and medieval chroniclers state that both catapult and ballista were used to throw stones and arrows, classification based on payloads is somewhat pointless. On the other hand, a great deal of insight can be gained through an investigation of the various propulsive mechanisms. Before the introduction of cannon, all artillery could be divided into three categories: those which worked by tension, by torsion, and by counterweight (counterpoise). Of the three types, we will find that tension engines are most often in the form of the outsize-arbalest and the springald. Our look at the torsion engines will involve the mangonel (most commonly called a catapult) and the ballista. Finally, we will discuss counterweighted engines such as the perrier and trebuchet. Although other sorts of siege engines were undoubtedly devised, and possibly even constructed, they were probably no more than variations on one of these three main categories.

In addition to names identifying the category into which a siege engine fell, nicknames were often coined for individual machines that had become particularly popular among the soldiery. In the same way pilots and crew of World War II bombers gave their planes names like Lady "B" Good, Lucky Doll, and Tiger Lady, medieval engineers and their crews christened their own favorite weapons of mass destruction with monikers like "war-wolf," "wild-cat," "bull-slinger," "ill-neighbor," "bad kinsman," "the queen," "the lady," and so forth. Their reasons for anthropomorphizing siege engines were probably identical to those of modern military men; it made the crew feel a part of something special, and it gave a very real identity to the piece of equipment in which the crew trusted their lives, safety, and hopes for success.

TENSION ENGINES:

OUTSIZE-ARBALEST AND SPRINGALDS

Tension engines function through the natural ability of wood to act like a spring—in the way a longbow acts like a spring when it looses an arrow. In fact, the most common form of tension engine was the outsized-arbalest, which was, in effect, a giant crossbow. In many ways, the outsize-arbalest resembles a ballista, which we will look at shortly, but its propulsive power comes from an entirely different mechanism.

Outsize-arbalest were popular enough that even Leonardo da Vinci, engineering genius that he was, designed a mammoth tension engine in the form of an arbalest. It is doubtful that the monstrous weapon was ever constructed, and less likely that it would have been very effective if it had been, but da Vinci's design serves as a clear example of how the mechanism worked as well as the popularity of the concept.

The only other well-known type of tension engine was a curious device called the

This monstrous wheel-mounted cross-bow, known as an outsize-arbalest, was designed by Leonardo da Vinci. Although it is an interesting idea, it is unlikely that such a contraption was ever built.

springald. The spear-throwing springald fired when a vertical plank was pulled back and released, allowing it to strike or slap a projectile, theoretically sending it hurtling toward its intended target. This technology is nothing more complicated than what every schoolboy has discovered by bending back a ruler and slapping it at a wad of paper. Although it may be a satisfactory means of annoying other students, basic physics and the law of diminishing returns make it impractical to apply the same principle to sending a spear hurtling through the air with enough power to do any noticeable damage beyond the first twenty or thirty feet. The springald certainly could not have thrown large enough projectiles to threaten the stout fortification walls of a town or castle. Unfortunately, such limitations constitute a recurring problem in much medieval military technology.

Hollywood tends to envision the basic catapult as a variation on the springald. A live tree gets bent backwards with the help of ropes or a winch, and when released, the tree springs forward sending a rock hurtling toward the bad guys, or launching the hero over the castle wall. Unfortunately, things don't work that way in real life. Any tree large enough to throw such heavy objects any distance would be far too thick to be bent. Even the name "catapult" has been distorted virtually beyond recognition. The term "catapult" has been applied to so many different projectile engines—both stone throwers and bolt throwers, those driven by tension and torsion, from the grandest trebuchet to the humblest slingshot—that it is useless as a term of classification. "Catapult" has become no more than a generic term describing any missile-throwing siege engine. In actuality, a catapult (or more accurately a mangonel) is a torsion-powered weapon capable of delivering a small payload a great distance, or a great payload a small distance.

This unlikely-looking machine, a mangonel-like version of the springald, was also drawn by da Vinci. It is doubtful that any wooden arm could have been bent with sufficient flex to provide the motive power to make the machine deliver its payload.

TORSION ENGINES:
MANGONEL AND BALLISTA

As early as the height of the Roman Empire, engineers understood that a torsion coil (a primitive version of the spring) could produce much more propulsive force than a bent piece of wood. The physics behind the torsion engine are exactly the same as those operating when you flick peas across the dining table with a spoon. Unlike the ruler described in the previous example, the spoon doesn't actually bend; instead it has an equal amount of forward and reverse force applied to it by a thumb and forefinger. When the spoon is drawn back and released, torsion snaps the spoon back to its original position. Ancient and medieval engineers applied torsion to their siege engines with the help of tightly wound coils of rope that held the firing arm in place and provided propulsive force when the machines were cocked. As mentioned before, torsion engines took two primary forms: the mangonel (catapult) and the ballista.

The mangonel's throwing arm was driven by a twisted skein of heavy rope or animal sinew[20] anchored to the outer frame of the engine and twisted—like a rubber band-powered airplane—until the rope was as tight as possible. For the engine to fire properly, the coil must be wound toward the front of the machine, the direction of the intended target. As the skein of rope is twisted into place, pressure forces the throwing arm against a crossbar at the top of the frame. The engine is cocked by pulling the

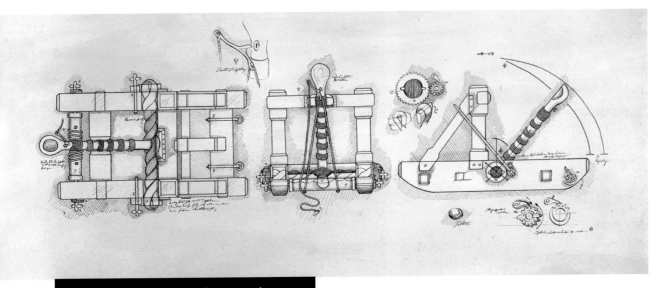

Based on ancient technology, the mangonel was capable of delivering a payload weighing 10 to 20 pounds up to 500 yards. Powered by simple torsion, neither the weight of the missile, nor the distance it could be thrown, could be increased to any great extent by enlarging the machine.

throwing arm downward, away from the crossbar, where it is locked into position on the base of the frame. When a stone or other projectile has been loaded onto the throwing arm, a catch is pulled, releasing the twisted rope and forcing the arm back to its original position against the crossbar and throwing the projectile up to 500 yards. With so great a firing range, the mangonel is safely beyond the reach of any bowman or slinger, so the real contest can quickly become one of siege engine versus siege engine.

At the siege of Acre in 1191, Richard of Devizes and Geoffrey de Vinsauf recorded the following incident:

> *The king of France turned his attention to the construction of machines for throwing stones... and he had one of superior quality to which they gave the name 'Bad Neighbor.' The Turks also had one they called 'Bad Kinsman,' which by its violent casts, often broke 'Bad Neighbor' to pieces.*

With these machines, one can, in fact, distinguish between light and heavy artillery. The size of the missile was not the decisive criterion, but rather the range obtained. Machines with particularly long throwing arms (between twenty-five and thirty feet) could be placed on a tower, their loading ends on the ground. When released, this vast beam would jerk upwards with tremendous force sending its stone ball far into the interior of the fortress.

As with the mangonel, the ballista is powered by twisted skeins of rope, hair, or sinew, but whereas the mangonel fires its payload in an overhead arc, the ballista sends its projectile along a horizontal path. Although the ballista may appear to be almost identical to the outsize-arbalest, the propulsive mechanism is very different. Here, there is no "bow" to be bent, but rather two independent arms are forced against a rigid frame with the aid of two torsion coils, very much like two small mangonels working in tandem.

The viciously effective ballista was an ideal weapon for use in the siege because it was

As they prepare for the approach of the English, the French bring a collection of siege weapons out of storage and assemble them in the castle's middle and outer bailey yards.

Although limited in capacity and distance, if calibrated properly the mangonel can serve as an effective antipersonnel weapon.

The French commander and his knights watch test firings of the siege engines. Disdainful of such machines, and the commoners who operate them, they realize that if they are to drive the hated English from the gates of their castle they must stoop to the same tactics as their enemy.

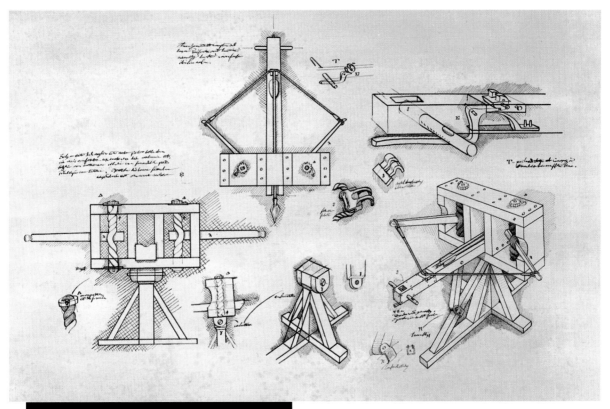

Much like a giant crossbow, the ballista could hurl a steel-tipped, javelinlike bolt several hundred yards. Light, maneuverable, and strong enough to rip a fully armored knight off his horse and pin him to a tree, the ballista was an ideal antipersonnel weapon.

both maneuverable and accurate. Constructed in a variety of sizes, some operated by a single man, others requiring a crew of half dozen, the ballista suited itself to a variety of tactics. Large field ballista could wreak havoc inside a castle compound by sending bolts the size of small telegraph poles crashing through the roofs of towers and buildings. Smaller models were equally effective as antipersonnel weapons, firing a five-foot javelin with an eighteen-inch iron head, which could plow through four or five men at a time or, in at least one instance, tear a fully armored knight from his horse and nail him to a tree. At the siege of Paris in 885, the sight of four men skewered by a single ballista bolt raised the remark that they

be taken to the kitchens and cooked like so many fowl on a spit.

Because they were both lightweight and maneuverable, ballista made ideal counteroffensive artillery when they were mounted on castle walls and towers. From the vantage point of a wall walk or tower, they could fire on enemy engines or siege towers and destroy them, or at least make it too dangerous to bring them within operating range of the castle. Ballista were especially successful when used as castle defenses because the height of a wall walk or tower added to their functional range.

The main drawback to torsion engines lies in their inconsistency. With repeated use, the torsion coil will slacken, decreasing the range of the weapon. Environmental factors will also change its performance. Rain can slacken the ropes to the point where they are useless. Even minor weather changes can affect

English soldiers, knights, and men-at-arms make easy targets for the ballista mounted in the towers of the French castle. From here, these giant, torsion-driven crossbows can fire nearly twice a minute into the ranks of the enemy.

Requiring two men to cock, the ballista is far more powerful than the largest crossbow, and far more deadly.

Firing with the kick of a mule, the ballista can easily skewer two or three men with a single shot.

their performance; torsion coils that are wet with the morning dew will behave differently than they did the previous afternoon. Nevertheless, torsion engines were relatively small, powerful, and easy to construct. They were very popular for delivering relatively small payloads over a great distance, but against the stout fortifications of a castle, considerably more force was required.

COUNTERPOISE ENGINES:

PERRIER AND TREBUCHET

The Greek mathematician Archimedes once said that given a long enough lever and a place to stand, he could move the world;

so it was a well-established fact by the Middle Ages that if a heavy weight had to be moved, a lever was the best solution. From this simple premise, two masterful siege engines were developed: the perrier and the trebuchet. Unlike all of the weapons we have looked at until know, these were not based on ancient Roman or Greek technology.[21]

The Arabs of the thirteenth century used an engine with a long seesaw-like throwing arm mounted on a rigid frame; it was discharged either by a gang of men or a team of horses.[22] This came to be known throughout Europe as a perrier. By pulling on ropes attached to one end of the pivoting arm, the opposite end was lifted into the air. If the pull was carried out with enough force, the opposing end would hurl a projectile in a forward arc.

With a large enough throwing arm and enough downward force, objects of almost unlimited size could be launched over impressive distances. Without getting into complicated

Above: Engineers labor to winch the massive tre-buchet arm down into position. The trebuchet was easily the most powerful and reliable artillery engine in the medieval arsenal.

Right: Although it requires a minimal amount of materials and technology to build, the perrier helps the English bring the battle 'home' to the French.

Even this small perri-er is easily capable of delivering a thirty- to forty-pound payload a distance of several hundred yards. This gives the English the ability to shatter the hoardings on the castle walls.

Unlike most other weapons in the medieval arsenal, the massive trebuchet operated by counterweight rather than torsion. As a result, the size of the payload that it could deliver, and the distance it could be thrown, could be increased almost indefinitely. Some trebuchet were known to have had a throwing arm of sixty-five feet in length and a counterweight in excess of three tons.

formulas, suffice it to say that a great deal of downward force is required to launch even moderately sized projectiles any real distance. Recently, a number of perrier of this design have been built to throw everything from cars to pianos for no particular reason other than the fact that it is fun and looks good on television. In these experiments, the power of men and horses has been replaced by a tractor or truck. To launch something the weight of a piano with a perrier, a medieval commander would need a team of about a hundred men or several dozen horses. Although it could be done, the cost in terms of manpower and resources would be prohibitive.

To compensate for the limited power of muscle, medieval military engineers took a cue from their architectural counterparts. Observing that counterweighted drawbridges were easier to raise than those simply winched closed with a windlass and muscle power, engineers developed a decisive improvement over the perrier. The new weapon was known as the trebuchet. It was also known as the terror of siege warfare.

On the trebuchet, the firing arm pivoted on a cross brace at a point only about a quarter of the distance from its butt end. The butt of the firing arm was weighted with measured weights that had been carefully calibrated for

When the massive trebuchet is brought into action, the direction of the battle changes dramatically. With a counterweight of over 1,200 pounds, this particular machine is capable of sending a 150-pound stone ball crashing into the castle. Although it may not be able to knock down the main curtain walls of the fortress, repeated assault can destroy almost any building within the compound.

dancer and the force of a sledgehammer.

Because the trebuchet operates on the principle of counterweight and gravity, its size and power can be increased almost indefinitely. Large trebuchets had throwing arms over sixty feet in length, carried counterweights of up to 20,000 pounds, and could launch missiles weighing nearly 600 pounds. The reconstruction shown to the left is located at the Middelaldercentret Center for Historical Technology in Denmark. It has a ballast of 33,600 pounds and is designed to throw projectiles weighing 350 pounds. Designed according to surviving medieval technology, the entire engine can pivot to change its firing direction. When loaded, the machine weighs around 47,000 pounds.

The possible effects of such punishing bombardment were seen as early as the siege of Acre in 1191, where a chronicler noted: "The templars and Hospitlars had... an engine... by means of which a part of the tower and wall of the castle [of the Saracens] were at length shaken down." Geoffrey de Vinsauf recorded the following about the siege of Acre:

At the Siege of Acre in 1189–91, the King of France had a petraria [stone thrower]... which by constant blows, broke down a wall

range. On the opposite end of the arm, a loose sling held the payload. To fire the trebuchet, the sling end of the arm was winched to the ground, allowing the sling to be loaded. When the stone or other projectile had been secured in the sling, the catch was released, allowing the weights to drop. As the weight descended, the firing arm arched high into the air where the sling automatically released, sending the payload toward its target with grace of a ballet

This giant trebuchet used walking wheels to winch down the throwing arm. The men inside the wheel would walk around its inner circumference, turning it like a hamster's exercise wheel. Machines of this size could require the men in the wheel to walk as much as a mile and a half to bring the arm into the locking position.

of the city. At the same siege one of the engines belonging to King Richard of England killed twelve men at one shot. This latter incident astonished the Saracens so much that they brought the stone ball to Saladin for inspection.

First used in Italy at the end of the twelfth century, the trebuchet was already widely employed in the Albigensian Crusade early in the following century. It made its appearance in England in 1216, during the siege of Dover by Prince Louis of France. The following year, a trebuchet was carried on one of Louis's ships when his fleet, attempting to enter the mouth of the Thames, was decisively defeated at the Battle of Sandwich: the machine, weighing down the ship "so deep in the water that the deck was almost awash," proved to be more of a handicap than an advantage.

The effectiveness of a trebuchet in a siege was formidable because of its capacity to hit the same target repeatedly with frightening precision. In 1244 Bishop Durand of Albi designed a trebuchet for the siege of Montségnur that hurled a succession of missiles weighing 88 pounds at the same point in the wall day and night, at twenty-minute intervals, until it battered an opening that rendered the fortress indefensible.

When England's King Edward I besieged the Scot-held Stirling Castle in 1304, he took along a trebuchet so large that it reportedly took a crew of fifty carpenters and five foremen several weeks to construct. Its disassembled parts had been transported to the siege in a train of thirty wagons and in the holds of three ships. Unfortunately, the besieged surrendered Sterling before the great machine, nicknamed "War-wolf," could be assembled. Not to be discouraged, Edward—aptly known as the "hammer of the Scot"—ignored the surrender, sealed off the castle, and bombarded the frantic Scots anyway.

The remarkable trebuchet was also effective as an antiweapon weapon. With their tremendous range and impressive throwing capacity, if the engineers could accurately gauge the distance of an enemy's siege weapon, they were likely to be able to knock it out of commission. Froissart recounts how, at the siege of Montagne in 1340, the trebuchet inside the walled city broke the throwing arm of the besiegers engine on the third shot. According to Froissart:

*Within Montagne there was a connying
maister in making of engyns who saw well
how the engyn of Valencens did greatly greve
them: he raysed an engyn in ye castle, the
which was not very great by he trymmed it to
a point, and he cast therewith but three
tymes. The first stone fell a [foot] from the
engyn without, the second fell on ye engyn,
and the thirde stone hit so true that it brake
clene asonder the shaft of the engyn without.*

PROJECTILES

The earthshaking din of boulders thundering off castle walls was always appreciated as a psychological weapon, intended as much to spread panic and terror as to do physical damage to the castle's defenses. On smaller fortresses, stone missiles may have been able to accomplish both purposes, but royal castles—with walls twenty or more feet thick—could withstand tremendous punishment. Indeed, the hardened soldiers inside a major castle under bombardment were as likely to receive the battering with scorn as with fear. It was not uncommon for a soldier standing near the spot where a trebuchet ball had impacted the parapets to lean over and pretend to wipe the dust from the wall. But it had taken time for the castle to catch up with the technology of the trebuchet.

As siege engines developed, castle walls improved to keep pace with them. In the early twelfth century, most curtain walls could still be battered down with concentrated fire, and they often were. But over the next century and a half, military architecture caught up with field technology, and castles again became havens of relative safety. There were, however, two equally effective strategies used by tacticians intent on bombarding a fortress. One was to throw things directly at the walls; the other was to throw things *over* the walls.

Because trebuchets can throw objects weighing several hundred pounds, they were routinely used to deliver a far broader range of payloads than just stones. It became common practice to lob the stinking carcasses of horses, sheep, and even human beings over castle walls in the hope of spreading disease and fear among the captive defenders.[23] In another instance of creative bombardment, two thousand cart loads of manure were heaved over the walls of the fortress of Carolstein in 1422. Anything that might spread disease or panic among a defending force was liable to become airborne in the hope that it would persuade the besieged to surrender.

At the siege of Auberoche, an emissary from the defending camp was sent out to meet the enemy with terms of surrender. As a graphic expression of the total unacceptability of the proposal, the besiegers used one of their trebuchets to fling the ambassador back over the walls of the castle. The entire grisly proceedings were recorded in the *Chronicles* of Jean de Froissart:

*To make it more serious, they took the varlet
and hung the letters round his neck and
instantly placed him in the sling of an engine
and then shot him back into Auberoche. The
varlet arrived dead before the knights who
were there and who were astonished and discomfited when they saw him arrive.*

To successfully hurl a man with a trebuchet, he would probably have to be tied into a bundle with ropes first so that he could be loaded into the throwing sling. One assumes that he would not willingly submit to such humiliation.

If a besieging army were unhappy with a messenger, or his message, but were not fortunate enough to have a trebuchet, they might use a mangonel to fling just the severed head of

When an English spy is sent into the castle, it is not long before he is captured by the French.

Left: After a ruthless interrogation, and a merciless beating, the spy is unceremoniously beheaded in front of the jeering French garrison.

Above: As a lesson to the English, the severed head of the spy is hurled over the castle walls and back into the English camp.

This line drawing, adapted from an illuminated manuscript of 1229, shows Crusaders using a perrier-like machine to throw the severed heads of captured enemy soldiers into the Turkish-held fortress of Nicea. Dead animals and human body parts were frequently used to spread disease in the hope of bringing the siege to a rapid conclusion.

any surface and was nearly impossible to extinguish even when it was submerged in water. The only modern equivalent to Greek fire is napalm, the horror of the Korean and Vietnam wars.

In 674 A.D. the city of Constantinople was in desperate straits, surrounded by the Islamic armies of the caliphs of Damascus. Fortunately, a savior was at hand in the unlikely form of a Syrian architect and alchemist named Callinicus. He was the inventor of Greek fire—the secret weapon of the Byzantine Empire, whose formula was so closely guarded that its precise ingredients are still unknown. Thanks to Callinicus's invention, the besieging fleet was utterly destroyed by a massive onslaught of Greek fire, and for another eight centuries, Byzantium remained safe from eastern invaders.

Later military writers, such as the thirteenth-century Mark the Greek, let it slip that Greek fire contained sulfur, saltpeter, oil, pine resin, and gum resin. It was delivered to its target either by being squirted over the enemy through a pump, which had to be recharged between each burst, or poured into pots or small kegs and launched by catapult or trebuchet. Supposedly, vats of the stuff were once kept below decks of ships and squirted through bilge pumps across the sides and decks of approaching enemy ships. However the Greek fire was delivered, its effects were horrific. The flaming, oil-based liquid floated on the surface of the water, setting fire to ship's hulls and frying any unfortunate sailors who hoped to save themselves by jumping into the sea. Inside castle compounds, these fire bombs landed like the wrath of God among crowds of people, groups of tethered horses, and on the thatched

the messenger back at the opposition, frequently with the terms of surrender nailed to his skull. An illustration from the thirteenth century *Histoires d' Outremer* clearly shows crusaders catapulting the severed heads of their captives over the walls of a besieged town.

GREEK FIRE

The more grisly payloads notwithstanding, one of the most effective uses of siege engines was the delivery of a highly flammable material known as Greek fire, a gelatinous terror weapon so sticky it would cling to almost

From the sixteenth-century work *Pirotechnia*, by Vannoccio Biringuccio, comes this later-period recipe for producing Greek fire:

One part each Grecian pitch [probably bitumen], alchitran, live sulfur, tartar, sarocolla, niter, and petroleum oil, and two parts quicklime. Mix them together with oil of egg yolk, place the mixture in a covered earthenware vessel, and bury it in a pile of warm manure for a month. After a month, put the covered earthenware vessel on the low fire until the mixture is liquefied. Pour the liquid into hollow sticks or small pots and place a fuse in the middle. Allow the Greek fire to cool.

The following is the liquid **Greek fire** of legend, supposedly flammable enough to ignite simply from being exposed to the direct rays of the sun:

Equal parts camphor, oil of sulfur, turpentine oil, elaterite oil [laterum oleum], juniper oil, rock oil, linseed oil, alchitran, finely crushed colophony, oil of egg yolk, pitch, Zagora wax, strained duck fat, saltpeter. Mix the ingredients with twice their volume of aqua vitae and an eighth part of the whole of arsenic and tartar and some sal ammoniac. Put the mixture into a covered earthenware pot and bury it under warm manure for two months. Then put the mixture in a retort and distill it over a slow fire. Within seven or eight hours, a liquid will be produced. Into this, put enough dried, pulverized cow dung to give it as much body as a heavy sauce.

roofs of barns and outbuildings. Froissart describes its effects at the siege of Breteuil:

Then they began to fire their engines and to fling fire on the top of the tower and inside it. The fire, which was Greek fire, set the roof of the tower alight, forcing men in it to abandon it hurriedly to save themselves from being burnt to death. Many were killed and wounded and the others were so harassed that they did not know which way to turn.

One of the few reliable means of extinguishing Greek fire seems to have been to douse the spreading flames with stale urine or strong vinegar. Apparently fresh urine contains too much ammonia to be effective, and the soldiery simply couldn't be expected to "produce" on command. Consequently, from the moment a prolonged siege seemed imminent, soldiers on both sides would begin relieving themselves in buckets and barrels against the possibility that it might be needed. Since both sides were capable of initiating a horrendous conflagration, all exposed woodwork and thatched roofs were protected by animal hides repeatedly soaked down with stale urine. In a matter of days the acrid stench of urine became overpowering (the smell was feared to carry noxious disease-bearing vapors). It rapidly became

With the French and English both using large-scale siege weapons, the battle becomes a constant terror. Round after round are delivered into the two camps as teams of engineers try to destroy each others' siege weapons and damage the enemy. Photo courtesy of Middlealdercentret, Denmark

apparent to both sides that the business of siege warfare was a far cry from the heroic ideals praised by the troubadours.

Back at our own siege, it seems unlikely that the English will be able to batter down the main walls of the French-held castle with their siege engines. Realizing this, they have begun to concentrate their artillery fire on one particularly vulnerable-looking corner tower. In a desperate attempt to hold back the English tide, the French have managed to destroy three English siege engines. As a result, the English are left with only two trebuchet and a perrier in operation. The wall-mounted French ballista have been well manned and used, but the attackers are undaunted. English engineers set to work rebuilding the damaged engines and

constructing still more devices with which to harass the French.

Despite their best efforts, the English have been unable to effect the strength of the walls or to do any real damage to the two large mangonel, which return fire from the safety of the castle compound. But they have been able to damage the corner tower. Having first set the roof aflame with Greek fire, the English trebuchet then managed to target a number of heavy boulders on the upper level. After suffering so much damage, the tower is unsafe, and the French are forced to abandoned it. In the overall scheme of siege warfare, this may seem a small victory, but it is an important one. With the tower undefended, the attackers have a clear line of approach to the base of the curtain wall, where sappers, miners, and ramming parties can work in relative safety to undermine a section of foundation. But the French see the direction English strategy seems to be taking and are equally determined to thwart the enemy's efforts.

Chapter Eight

ATTACKING THE FOUNDATIONS

Ramming, Sapping, and Mining

The English now gauge their options carefully. They find themselves with a clear approach to an undefended section of wall and the base of the corner tower, but they are no closer to routing the French. How, then, can they best exploit the vulnerability in the castle defenses? Their options remain the same as always: over the wall, under the wall, or through the wall. Knowing that the wall has already suffered some degree of structural damage from the constant pounding, the next tactical phase will be directed toward opening a breach and going through the wall. With a relatively clear line of approach to the base of the tower and adjoining sections of wall, the English now concentrate on destroying the castle's underpinnings.

RAMMING

In terms of form and function, the two siege machines that remained most consistent throughout the Middle Ages were the battering ram and the bore. Nearly identical weapons were used in the sixth century at the siege of Rome and five hundred years later, during the First Crusade in the eleventh century when Godfrey of Boullion besieged and captured Jerusalem. The ram and bore were used during the peasant risings of the sixteenth century and even as late as 1705, when Bavarian peasants tried to take Munich in a vain bid to expel the Austrians during the Wars of the Spanish Succession.

The reason for the longevity of these devices was their pure simplicity. They were easily built, required no sophisticated engineering knowledge, and were frequently quite effective. The theory behind their use is equally simple. If you want to break a stone, use a hammer or a chisel.

The purpose-built hammer was the battering ram: an enormous timber, such as a heavy beam or tree trunk, slung beneath a framework (or penthouse) of stout beams and fitted with an iron head. Although small hand-held rams were certainly used, they were only effective for battering down a door or gate, not for breaching stout masonry walls. Whether hand-held or suspended in a frame, rams were swung repeatedly against the same section of wall until the masonry cracked and finally dislodged. Both ram and bore were normally concealed under a protective wooden canopy, called a "sow," to protect the ramming party while they were working. The roof of the sow was covered in fresh animal hides to combat fire arrows or combustible mixtures thrown from above.

The chisel of our metaphor was the bore: a heavy, metal pole with a point on one end.[24] Bores were used to break individual stones loose from the wall, until a hole and finally a breach had been made.[25] Its action earned it the name "musculus," because it gnawed away at defensive walls like a mouse. Both ram and bore were "slung by ropes or

Taken from a nineteenth-century illustration, we see a variety of ramming tactics and countermeasures used to thwart their effectiveness. Under the protection of sows, ramming parties approach the walls of a fortress, while defenders lower rush mattings, wooden hurdles, and bags of sand to absorb the shock of the ram. On the far left a wooden beam will be used to snag the head of the ram or to break its shaft.

The success of ramming against castle doors led entry gates to become the most highly protected point along the outer wall. Guarded by flanking towers and drawbridges, the castle gate presented a daunting obstacle to would-be invaders. These flanking towers and accompanying defenses were well designed for deadly effectiveness. Outside and inside, the barbican presented the most brutal of killing fields. Should an assault party break through the gate in an attempt to gain access to the outer bailey yard of the castle, they would be trapped inside the passage when the portcullis was dropped behind them or if the drawbridge was raised. Once trapped, the attackers, sealed between two fortified assault towers, could quickly be cut down by a hail of arrows.

chains from two perpendicular beams, drawn back by the workers as far as the chains allowed and then needed to dash itself against the wall." The advantage of the bore was that it required only a few hands to manipulate it, whereas up to sixty men were required to rhythmically swing the huge beam of a ram. On the other hand, the bore, slowly chipping away at the mortar joins between massive stone blocks, made discouragingly slow progress.

Ram and bore are just two names describing a broad general category of battering machines. Certainly, there existed a bewildering variety of "ram heads" and bore designs, but the function was inevitably limited to either smashing and cracking masonry with blunt-force trauma, or chipping away at mortar to loosen individual blocks.

The effectiveness of both ram and bore depended on the ability of the besiegers to outwit those defending the enemy fortress. When Godfrey de Bullion attacked Jerusalem, he had the moat filled in at the location where he wanted a battering ram erected. To protect the crew from the arrows and missiles of the defenders, he covered the ram with a strong roof, but despite the protective roofing, and later protective sides (virtually enclosing the ram inside a

house), it was still not entirely safe. Raw hides, tiles, and the like could only resist Greek fire, pitch, or other liquid combustibles for a limited period. Consequently, the protective house had to be put on wheels so the crew could withdraw and repair the damage between attacks. (Some late medieval illustrations even portray rams without rams; consisting of a wedge-shaped shed, with its pointed end clad in iron and the entire structure set on wheels ready to be driven headlong against the wall.[26])

At our siege, the English are ready to push their ram to a spot along the castle wall most likely to prove vulnerable to its work. The great wooden doors of the gate house would seem the most obvious target, but they are so heavily guarded that a safe approach is almost impossible. Knowing this, the English were scouting for a more likely place to position the ramming party.

Thanks to the effective work of the English artillery engines inflicting damage on the walls and hoardings around the corner tower, the English have a vulnerable spot that has become almost impossible for the French to defend. This does not mean the English will have an easy time. Although the hoardings have been broken and the upper floors of the

An English ramming party assaults the main gate of the middle ward with a small, hand-held battering ram.

When the wooden draw-bar holding the gate shatters under the force of the ramming, English knights and men-at-arms surge forward.

In bloody hand-to-hand fighting, English attackers and French defenders struggle for control of the gate house.

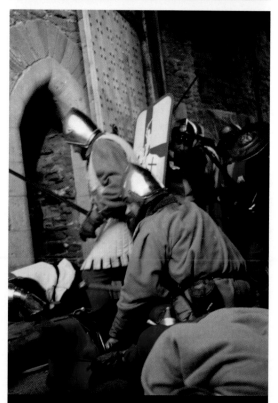

The French put up a valiant fight but are no match for the overwhelming numbers of the English.

tower abandoned, the wall itself remains a serious obstacle. This particular section of wall may be almost unguarded, but its base has been reinforced with an additional course of stone as an added deterrent.

This extra layer of masonry is often referred to as a rampart specifically because their bases are angled outward to deflect and absorb the shock of a battering ram. Furthermore, any missiles dropped from above will ricochet off the slanted surface of the rampart and into the face of the ramming party. To even approach the wall, the rammers must get across the moat, and building a causeway across a moat can prove dangerous and time-consuming work. Froissart describes such an endeavor during the siege of Breteuil in 1356:

> The peasants in the district were ordered to
> bring great quantities of wood and logs and
> unload them into the moats, and then spread
> straw and dirt on top so that the [engine]
> could be wheeled against the walls to assault
> the defenders....

As the English press through the gate house and into the outer ward, French guards in the gate house tower use a sluice port to shower the enemy with quicklime, which filters through chain mail and visors, burning flesh and eyes.

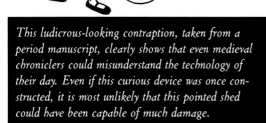

This ludicrous-looking contraption, taken from a period manuscript, clearly shows that even medieval chroniclers could misunderstand the technology of their day. Even if this curious device was once constructed, it is most unlikely that this pointed shed could have been capable of much damage.

Once the rammers actually find a way to assault the wall, they hope the shock of the ram, alternated with continued assault from perrier and trebuchet, can be concentrated in one area long enough to dislodge the heavy stones of the wall. But it may take weeks before they can tell for certain whether or not their work has been successful, and during that time, their lives are in constant peril.

The constant press of the ramming party does not go unanswered by the French.

Arrows, boiling water, red-hot iron pellets, quicklime, sand, and even stones torn from the battlements cascade down on the roof of the sow as it nears the wall.[27] If the sow and its occupants are not crushed by missiles from above as they approach the wall, massive wicker mats will be lowered down the face of the wall to absorb the shock of the ram. Logs, timbers, looped ropes, or grappling hooks will all be used to snare and inhibit the movement of the ram head.

By the beginning of the fourteenth century, there had been a noticeable decline in references to rams and bores as methods of breaching a wall. On the other hand, picks, mauls, hammers, mason's axes, chisels, wedges, and trowels continued to form a normal part of an army's siege train—all of which suggests that mining remained as important as ever.

SAPPING AND MINING

If an attacking army had the luxury of continuing a siege for months, a different and often more effective strategy of capturing a castle was frequently employed. A common weakness of castle defenses lay in their subsoil. Unless a castle was founded wholly on solid rock, some point along its walls was vulnerable to mining. Sinking a tunnel or mine (as it was called in medieval military parlance) beneath the walls of a castle was devastatingly effective.

Mining, though often successful, was a slow operation. It was impossible where a castle was built on marshy or wet ground, or on solid rock, and sometimes breaches in the curtain walls created by mining operations were filled up again overnight by the desperate defenders. Nevertheless, the undermining of walls and towers played a major role in siege craft.

The mine would be directed toward a section of wall most likely to prove vulnerable, such as a corner of the curtain wall or a square tower. Corners, by their nature, are structurally weak. During King John's siege of Rochester Castle, he ordered nearby Canterbury to manufacture "by day and night as many picks as you are able." Following six weeks of digging, King John's miners were able to exploit the structural weakness of corners by first bringing down a section of the curtain wall and later by collapsing a corner of the great keep, where the garrison retreated after the collapse of the outer walls.[28]

Mining was slow and arduous work because mines had to be dug from a safe distance and shielded from sight, beneath a shed or hurdles, to ensure that the castle's defenders were kept ignorant of the miners' presence. If houses were scattered near the castle, one of these could easily be used to conceal the mine opening. As they drove their tunnels through dangerously unstable earth, miners used timbers and planks to prop up the ceiling and walls of the shaft to prevent collapse or subsidence, which would alert castle watchmen to the miners' work.

When the mine shaft reached a point directly beneath the castle wall, it was enlarged until it was the size of a small room. This chamber was supported by timbers soaked in tallow or pitch. The cavity was then packed with branches, brushwood, rags, grease, and hog carcasses—anything combustible. On the order from the sergeant of miners, the giant tinder box would be set ablaze. As the fire raged, the supporting timbers burned away, and the hog carcasses swelled and exploded, collapsing burning timbers, their grease serving to fuel the conflagration.

The destruction of the support beams,

ATTACKING THE FOUNDATIONS

hen King John of England besieged Rochester Castle in 1215—a vast twelfth-century keep defended by about a hundred rebel knights, a number of foot soldiers, and bowmen—he sent a letter to one of his knights, stating: "We command you, that with all haste, you send us forty of the fattest pigs of the sort least good for eating, to bring fire under the tower." From the early fifteenth century, barrels of gunpowder replaced hog carcasses as the explosive of choice, and from midcentury, zigzag passages were designed to protect retreating miners against the blast (undoubtedly a lesson learned through hard experience). In a Sienese manuscript from around 1470, there is even a reference to miners using a compass to keep them on course.

combined with the explosions, would generally drop the foundations of the wall into the mine shaft, sending huge sections of wall, along with men and equipment, crashing to the ground. Once such a breach had been made, the assault forces charged through smoke and rubble to engage the defenders in hand-to-hand combat.

The mine was perhaps the most lethal weapon in the besieger's store. Builders tried, where possible, to site their castles on solid rock or provide them with a deep, wet moat, both of which helped deter miners. Where such a site was lacking, the base of the curtain wall was sometimes splayed outward at the bottom

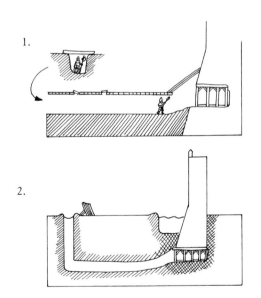

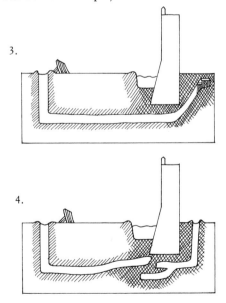

Here we see four of the most common mining tactics. 1. Miners approach the base of a tower by means of a covered trench. 2. A deep mine reaches the base of a wall, which is then propped up with timbers, ready to be set on fire. 3. A mine leading beyond a wall will allow a small party of men into the castle. 4. A countermine dug by defenders is about to break into an oncoming mine.

hen the Earl entered the town and laid siege around the castle, as near as he might, and reared up all his engines, the which cast night and day against the walls, but they did little hurt, the walls were so strong of hard stone; it was said that of old time it had been wrought by the hands of the Saracens, who made their works so strongly there is none such nowadays. When the earl saw he could do no good with his engines he caused them to cease; then he called to him his miners to the intent that they should make a mine under the walls, which was not soon made. Eleven weeks later the castle was still holding out.

So long wrought the miners that at last they came under the base court but under the donjon [keep] they could not get for it stood on hard rock. However in the meantime, the miners had brought down a tower in the outer bailey. The defenders, not realizing that the donjon was defeating every effort of the miners and would continue to do so, decided the end was at hand and that they should ask for terms. This was a gentlemanly occasion, and terms were granted; the castle surrendered and its occupants allowed to depart. On many similar occasions the end of the siege was the beginning of a bloody massacre.
— **Froissart, *Chronicles*, The Siege of Reole, 1345**

to thicken it. More rarely, a curtain wall was constructed with load-bearing arches along its length so that, should a part of the wall be undermined, the arch would prevent the collapse of an entire section of wall.

Occasionally a mine was driven beyond the wall itself so that during the night a small party of attackers could emerge inside the castle and open its gates.

Undermining the walls of a castle was a complicated procedure requiring the work of skilled specialists. Besieging forces eventually came to employ special units of experienced miners and engineers, who could select the spot most likely to succumb to mining. Although miners were counted among the most dangerous and effective weapons in siege warfare, theirs was a hazardous occupation almost entirely devoid of glory. Mining was seen as a job for peons, and those who engaged

in it were derisively referred to as peoneers or pioneers.[29] They were held in contempt not only by members of the chivalry (which is probably to be expected at this point) but by archers and engineers as well. Even a dog could dig a hole under a fence; no man of honor would fight a war in that fashion. In *The Life of King Henry V*, Shakespeare's Fluellen speaks of the mines at the siege of Harfleur:

To the mines! tell you the Duke, it is not so good to come to the mines; for look you, the mines is not according to the disciplines of war; the concavities of it is not sufficient; for look you, th'athversary, you may discuss unto the duke, look you, is digt himself four yard under the counter mines: by Cheshu, I think a' will plow up all, if there is not better directions.

Despite their lowly position within the military hierarchy, miners tenaciously and bravely gnawed away at the structural integrity of castle walls. Certainly castles on rocky hillsides or behind expansive water-filled moats presented difficult challenges, but given enough time, the miners could get the better of almost any wall, and they could prove just as effective above ground as beneath it.

Under the protection of sows, the English miners in our story work alongside their ramming teams. These above-ground miners, known as sappers, probe for weak spots in the castle walls and ramparts with picks and iron bars, attempting to disassemble the massive masonry defenses one stone at a time. Given even one spot in which to start their work—and enough time to complete the task—the sappers will open a hole in the wall of stone that surrounds the towering and intractable fortress.

Guillaume Le Breton wrote of the effectiveness of sappers at the siege of Chateau Gaillard: "The French then began sapping operations, under the protection of their shields, on the salient tower of the outer bailey

In addition to King John's siege of Rochester, mining brought the downfall of Chateau Gaillard, the massive citadel in Normandy built by John's brother, Richard I, with a three-bailey defense. King Philip of France laid siege to Chateau Gaillard in the late summer of 1203. He had once boasted that he would take the formidable castle "even if its walls were made of iron," to which the warrior King Richard had replied that he would hold it "were its walls made of butter." Alas, Richard was not there to defend the castle against Philip, having died in 1199. John attempted to relieve Chateau Gaillard but failed.

The siege continued throughout the winter and into the spring, when the French made a determined assault with mangonels and trebuchets; at the same time, they made a causeway across the wet moat, undermined the outer bailey wall, and breached it. Next the middle bailey wall was also taken. Finally a section of the inner bailey wall was battered and mined until it collapsed.

With great difficulty, a cavern was hallowed out under the curtain wall, the space was filled with props, brush wood and other combustibles—the intense heat under the hallowed-out foundations caused the wall to crack and fall. It produces a great roar as it collapses... a cloud of smoke whirls upwards in a twisting vortex with mixed flame and smoke and the ruin belches out a great dust cloud that mushrooms out above....

The castle's keep was captured, its occupants severely weakened by hunger. The fall of the great stronghold led to the loss of Rouen and all of John's possessions in Normandy.

English sappers chip a cavern into the base of a tower as they prepare to bring it to the ground.

and were successful in excavating a cavity, strutting, firing the timber, and in bringing down the tower. The outer bailey was then taken and the French proceeded to attack the remaining works." The passage "under the protection of shields" refers to the tactic of "tortoising," where sappers worked individually at the base of the wall probing for weaknesses while wearing large shields on their backs for protection, hence their likening to the hard-shelled reptile. A ram slung beneath a sow was also sometimes referred to as a tortoise due to its zoomorphic likeness to the creature, its head darting in and out of its shell. Usually, sappers worked under portable

This drawing, adapted from a medieval manuscript illumination, shows sappers working under the protection of a wheeled sow while defenders assault them with rocks and what appear to be bundles of burning straw.

sows set lengthwise along the wall, but some notable exceptions to this rule exist. Occasionally, sappers would unwisely work without any protective cover, as at Acre in 1191, where cash incentives offered by Richard I seem to be the only explanation for their suicidal behavior.

Obviously, the threat posed by miners and sappers was real and ever-present to a garrison under siege. There were few effective countermeasures. Mining presented a great danger to even the strongest of castles, and its effectiveness had been evident since ancient Greece. In the fifth century B.C., Herodotus wrote: "So the Persians besieged Barca for nine months in the course of which they dug several mines from their own lines to the walls. But their mines were discovered by a man who works in brass, who went with a brazen shield all around the fortress, and laid it on the ground inside the city... and where the ground was undermined, there the brass of the shield rung. Here, therefore, the Barcaens countermined and slew the Persian diggers." Although

the medieval Europeans are not known to have made use of vibrating shields, they did, on occasion, place pans of water on the ground and watch the surface of the water, which would ripple if the ground beneath it was disturbed. The obvious drawback to this method was that the water would only register the presence of miners once they were beneath the walls; no problem if the miners intended to tunnel into the castle and invade, but much too late if their intent was to bring down the wall.

Miners themselves were relatively safe from detection. The defenders of a castle in the process of being mined could only thwart approaching miners by building a second rampart behind the wall under attack, or by digging a countermine into the enemy tunnel, capturing it, and filling it back in. If a countermine was dug, it could lead to horribly cramped fighting in the most claustrophobic conditions.

Sometimes small shafts were sunk into the mines, from inside the castle or from counte mines, and the besieger's mine could be flooded with smoke or water to drive the miners out of their tunnel. At Coucy, a spring at ground level was used to flood an enemy mine simply by digging a drainage shaft into the approaching mine. But this could only be accomplished if careful observation identified the exact line of approach. Locating an oncoming mine was not

SIEGE OF NICAEA, 1097

Meanwhile the engines, pounding away at the walls, met with vigorous resistance from the garrison, who threw torches as well as pitch, oil, lard, and other inflammable materials at them, destroying a great number. One large tower offered great resistance, and after incessant attack by two siege engines not a stone was moved. At length, when more engines were brought up against it and larger and harder stone missiles employed, some fissures were made in its wall. The base of the wall was attacked by a battering-ram and by sappers with crowbars. But all these efforts were in vain, for the breaches made during the day were repaired by the garrison during the night. Eventually a very strong pent-house was built and brought up to the tower. Under the protection of this covering, on which flaming materials and huge rocks of stone were thrown without effect, sappers worked away at the base of the wall.

As the masonry at the base of the wall was removed by the sappers its place was supplied by props and stays, and when a cavity of sufficient size for their purpose had been made, combustible materials were thrown among the timber work. The men then set fire to the props and escaped back to the camp, leaving the pent-house where it was. At midnight, when the props were consumed, the tower fell with such a deafening crash that the sound could be heard from a great distance. After that event the citizens, realizing that their case was hopeless, surrendered themselves to the Emperor Alexios and the city was taken.

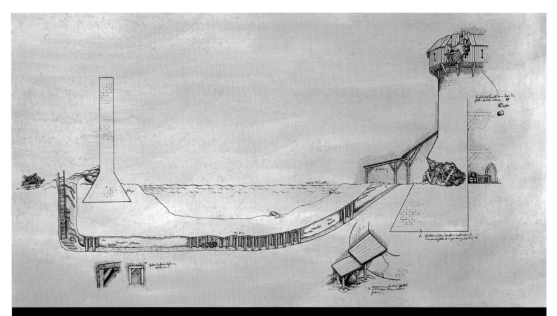

Here we clearly see the course of the English mine. Its opening hidden behind the outermost wall of the French fortress, the mine drops to a level well beneath the curtain wall, travels the width of the moat, and returns to the surface on the narrow ribbon of land just outside of the walls guarding the middle ward. Here, sappers and miners open a cavern hoping to bring down the wall, opening a breach by which the English can gain entrance to the fortress.

easy, and a countermine might itself further weaken the castle's walls. An attempt by the Franks to mine Dyrrachium (1108) was frustrated when the Greeks broke in and blew Greek fire through reed pipes into the faces of the enemy miners. Occasionally countermines were dug prior to a siege as a precautionary measure.

Examples of both mine and countermine still exist at St. Andrews Castle in Scotland. During the siege of 1546–47, the attacking forces drove an underground tunnel towards the castle from a point about 130 feet outside the walls. Countermining was then undertaken by the garrison and, after some tentative efforts to locate the advancing mine, eventually broke into it at a point almost midway between the walls and the starting point of the mine. The countermining was so exact that although the mine had deviated considerably from a straight course, the countermine broke into it at a level directly above the heads of the oncoming enemy.

Sometimes a desperate attempt was made

to plug a breach when mining operations brought down a section of curtain wall. At Dover in 1216, a section of the northern gate house, brought down by French miners, was filled with timber by Hubert de Burgh's men, who subsequently beat off the French. Two other mine-thwarting alternatives are illustrated by the siege of Carcassonne in 1240, as related in *Chanson de la Croisade Albigeoise.*

The attackers began a mine against the barbican gate of Narbonne. And forthwith, we, having heard the noise of their work underground, made a counter-mine, and constructed a great and strong wall of stones laid without the mortars in the inside of the barbican, so that we thereby retained full half of the barbican. When they set fire to the hole in such wise that the wood having burned out, a portion of the barbican fell down! The outer defense line, the barbican of Carcassonne, was then still constructed of wood.

They then began to mine against another turret of the lice; we counter-mined, and got possession of the hole which they had excavated. They therefore began to tunnel a mine between us and a certain wall and destroyed two embrasures of the lices. But we set up there a good and strong palisade between us and them.

They also started a mine at the angle of the town hall, near the bishop's palace, and by dint of digging from a great way off arrived at a certain Saracen wall, by the wall of the lices; but at once, when we detected it, we made a good and strong palisade between us and them, higher up the lices, and counter-mined. Thereupon they fired their mine and flung down some ten fathoms of our embrasure front. But we made hastily another good palisade with a brattice upon it and loopholes; so none among them dared to come near us in that quarter.

They also began a mine against the barbican of the Rodez Gate, and kept below ground, wishing to arrive at our walls, making a marvelous great tunnel. But when we perceived it we forthwith made a palisade on one side and the other of it. We counter-mined also, and having fallen in with them, carried the chamber of their mine.

Mining failed to take Carcassonne as did attacks from the outside, and with a relief force en route, the siege was eventually abandoned.

Although they failed as often as they succeeded, mines were so feared, that sometimes they achieved the desired result without ever being completed. When Lord Burghersh secretly drove a mine under the tower of the castle at Cormicy in France in the fourteenth century, he invited the knight in charge of the defenses to visit the work. The mere sight of the excavation caused the well-provisioned French to offer an immediate surrender. Lord Burghersh happily took the undamaged fortress into his possession and refilled the mine shaft.

Even when a castle's defenses were successfully softened up by mining, its actual seizure was still no foregone conclusion. It might be difficult to get enough men through a breach fast enough to be effective. Flanking fire from towers farther along the breached wall could cut down attackers, and often a rampart at the base of the breach made the last few feet awkward to scramble over and caused stones hurled from above to ricochet at unpredictable angles. Nevertheless, mining eventually became the most universally practiced method of attack. Once miners set to work, the collapse of a castle was simply a question of time.

At our siege, the English commander had counted on using his miners from the very beginning of the attack. They have been working their way toward the foundations of the fortress since the English first began to entrench themselves around the castle. Experienced miners, after carefully determining the most promising line of approach, had asked if artillery fire could be concentrated on one particular corner to weaken the defenses. The engineers coordinated their fire to work with the miners, and the tactic has proven successful. The mine is finished, and a chamber is hollowed out beneath the weakened masonry. The pioneers are ready to set fire to the mine. However, knowing the difficulty of getting an attacking force through a narrow and well-defended breach, the commander of the English forces has ordered the sergeant of miners not to fire the mine. It will be used, but not before another tactic can be brought into play.

Chapter Nine

OVER THE TOP

Siege Towers

The commander of the English force knows that even if the mine successfully opens a breech in the wall, getting enough men through the opening fast enough to overwhelm the French could be a problem. His plan, therefore, is to fire the mine in conjunction with a diversionary attack on the walls. Scaling parties will assault various points along the perimeter in conjunction with an attack by a massive siege tower—now under construction. With any luck, the defenders will be forced to concentrate their efforts on repelling the tower and the scalers, leaving the area around the mine nearly undefended. When the mine is fired, an English detachment should be able to force their way through the breach with little opposition. To this end, English engineers have been laboring for more than a week to construct the mobile siege tower.

If all other forms of attack failed to force a castle to surrender, medieval besiegers often attempted a final, more complex form of escalade. Wooden siege towers, as tall as the fortress walls, gave attackers direct access to the men on the parapet wall. Although complicated and time consuming to build, siege towers (or "belfries" as they were often called) became a common feature in major sieges throughout the Middle Ages. Belfries were divided into several floors with ladders or staircases running from the ground floor to a fighting platform atop the tower.[30]

The cumbersome towers were filled with men and equipment and slowly rolled toward the castle wall. Once in position, a drawbridge in the tower's face was lowered onto the parapet. The men inside the tower then charged across the bridge to engage the enemy on their own ground. William of Malmesbury, an English chronicler of the twelfth century, describes the use of a belfry by the crusaders during the siege of Jerusalem in July 1099:

The making of this machine delayed the siege, on account of the unskilfulness of the workmen and the scarcity of wood. And now the 14th day of July arrived when some men began to undermine the walls with the sows, others to move forward the tower. To do this more conveniently they took it toward the works in separate pieces and, putting it together at such distance as to be out of bow-shot, advanced it on wheels nearly close to the wall. In the meantime the slinger with stones, the archers and the crossbowmen began to press forward and dislodge their opponents from the ramparts. Soldiers unmatched in courage ascend the tower, waging nearly equal war against the enemy with missile weapons and with stones. Nor indeed were our foes at all remiss; but trusting their whole security to their valor, they poured

down grease... upon the tower.... During the whole of that day the battle was such that neither army seemed to think they had been worsted.[31]

Like so much medieval military hardware, the siege tower had been a familiar sight on the battlefields of the ancient world. Roman chronicles contain (highly improbable) accounts of siege towers that reached twenty stories in height. Obviously, the more imposing the walls of a castle, the taller and more unwieldy a siege tower would have to be to reach the top. One of the Anglo-Norman belfries constructed at Lisbon in 1147 was eighty-three feet high, and another was even larger at ninety-five feet. The towers built during crusader attacks on Tyre and Acre were said to be forty, fifty, and sixty cubits high.[32]

Siege towers were used by John II at Breteuil in 1356, and Henry V took them on his Agincourt campaign. The Turks used siege towers when they successfully overran Constantinople in 1453, and during the siege of Malta at Birgu in 1565.[33] Certainly the huge display of effort and energy required to build them made the belfry a favorite of almost everyone who took up the cross and went on crusade. The *Gesta Francorum* recounts the belfry employed at the siege of Jerusalem in 1099:

Then our commanders made arrangements for Jerusalem to be captured with siege-engines, so that our men could enter to worship at the Church of the Holy Sepulcher. They made two wooden siege-towers, and many other devices. Godfrey of Bouillon made his own siege-tower with machines in it, and so too did Raymond of Toulouse; the wood for these things had to be dragged from a considerable distance away.

The Saracens inside the city, seeing that

When a siege tower successfully reached the walls of an enemy castle, anxious knights would finally get their moment of glory, charging across the parapets to fight the enemy on even ground.

our men were making these devices, made remarkable improvements in its fortifications and had the towers nightly increased in height. When our leaders saw which part of the city was the weakest, one night they brought a wooden siege tower and a machine up to the eastern side. At the break of dawn they erected them, fitted out the siege-tower and equipped it for 3 days.

The scale of the attack described above gives an insight into the major drawback of the siege tower. Such immense projects could only be undertaken by kings and noblemen with almost limitless amounts of money and manpower at their disposal.

Obviously a tower had to reach the top of a fortified wall to be of any use. Occasionally they were constructed so that although the drawbridge was at parapet level, the top of the tower was higher still, allowing men on an upper platform to sweep the parapet clear of defenders while the men inside the tower surged onto the walls. A tower used at the siege of Tyre was tall enough that "one could look down into the city below." As belfries grew taller, castle walls and towers grew to match them. By the beginning of the fourteenth century, the towering walls of castles had reached a height that no siege tower could reasonably match. At Warwick Castle, Guy's Tower was raised to 128 feet while Caesar's Tower reached an even more impressive 147 feet. But few castles could boast such commanding defenses, so the siege tower continued to be an effective weapon in most instances.

Although the effectiveness of belfries was unquestionable, they were extremely complicated and expensive to build. The height of the tower had to be precise. If it was too low, the men on the fighting platform were vulnerable to attack and would be unable to reach the top of the walls. If the tower was too tall they would be too far above the wall walks to engage the defenders. In point of fact, most belfries only needed to be two or three stories in height to reach the top of a castle's outer curtain wall and, once in position, could pose a serious threat to the defenders. Roger of Wendover relates how, at the siege of Bedford in 1224, Henry III's belfry was so effective that no man inside the defenses dared to remove his armor

for fear that he would be shot dead. At Nicaea, on the First Crusade, a Lombard specialist was appointed master of the works because of his "marvelous skill" and was well paid for his efforts. Sailors, used to working in wood aboard ships, were often useful in constructing a variety of siege engines; at Jerusalem during the siege of 1099, they felled trees, smoothed timber, and fitted beams together for the engines, with "the speed of experienced carpenters."

Because of their size and bulk, towers were generally built on-site by a number of

The siege tower illustrated here clearly shows the complex design and engineering that went into such machines. The framework is set on wheels, making the tower mobile enough to be pushed to the walls of the castle. The exterior of the structure is covered with wood and sheathed in wet hides as a cautionary measure against fire, while the sloped roof is intended to deflect incoming missiles. Inside, the tower is divided into four floors, each of which can act as a fighting platform, the uppermost allowing archers to guard the drawbridge as it is lowered onto the walls of the enemy castle. The drawbridge is operated by means of a windlass located on the bottom floor of the tower.

crews, each led by an engineer responsible for an individual machine. It often took valuable time—eleven weeks at Tyre to make two towers and a ram. Frequently a heady spirit of competition developed between the teams over the size and ingenuity of their machines. Sometimes belfries could be put together with surprising speed. At the siege of Antioch, it seems to have been done in a few days. At Banyas "it seemed as if a tower had been suddenly erected in the very midst of the place." The tower built at Dorpat in 1224 was made from trees that stood as tall as the walls of the fortress and was built in only eight days. The same period was required by James I of Aragon's engineer Nicoloso in Majorca. According to an Italian chronicler, the Turks built a tower over the course of a night in 1453 so that it simply appeared the next morning "on the lip of the ditch." One suspects that some prefabrication was employed in this last instance. Whatever the case, the writer believed it would have taken the Christians a month to build such a tower.

Prefabrication of the massive component parts needed to construct a siege tower was not as unusual as it might seem. On numerous occasions, towers were built in advance and transported to the site of a siege, a method employed by Richard I during his crusading siege of Acre. Edward I brought a wooden tower to Bothwell and transported it from there to Stirling on thirty carts. In 1287, as part of one of his many campaigns against the Welsh, the same king provided an escort of twenty cavalry and 450 infantry to move a disassembled tower that was packed on wagons drawn by forty to sixty oxen, depending upon the difficulty of the terrain. A tower used at one of the sieges of Orléans during the Hundred Years' War required twenty-six carts to transport. King Louis of France needed 1,600 carts to carry his engines and provisions on his campaign of 1242, and the train stretched along the highway more than three miles.

Whether built in situ or transported to the site, belfries all had certain features in common. They were made of wood, mounted on

Not all siege towers were designed to be moved into position after they were completed. According to Roman chroniclers at the siege of Marseilles in 49 B.C., Julius Caesar built a stationary tower of brick—thirty feet square, six storeys in height, with walls five feet thick—under the very walls of the city, while daring a constant barrage of missiles from the defenders. When the ground floor was built, it was covered with a solid, fireproof roof, which was not secured to the walls but rested upon them like a lid. The eaves projected considerably, and from them, screens were hung to cover the walls below. By means of screws, the canopy of roof and screens could be raised one storey in height so that the workmen could continue to build up the walls of the tower one storey at a time in complete safety. This process was repeated until the tower reached the height of the fortified walls, at which time the Romans swarmed onto the parapets to face their enemies.

wheels or rollers, had several stories, and were sheathed with some sort of protection against the missiles and incendiary devices the enemy was likely to throw at them. A tower used at Sidon in 1110 had matting and fresh ox hides covering it, and at Acre, a tower was covered with skins soaked in vinegar and mud. Belfries made by Frederick Barbarossa for use in his campaigns in Italy were apparently sheathed in iron for protection, which must have added considerably both to their cost and weight. James I of Aragon described a wheeled tower that he covered "like a house" and pushed forward by poles; it was protected by three thicknesses of hurdles, with a roof of hurdles and brushwood, which was, in turn, covered with earth as a protection against stone-throwing engines.[34]

A particularly elaborate Turkish tower of 1453 was protected by earth, by bull and camel hides layered inside and out, and by turrets and protective barricades on top. The Anglo-Norman tower at Lisbon was covered with heavily woven collision mats, which were, in turn, draped with ox hides. Each layer of hides overlapped the one below, the tails of each hide dangling so that when water was poured from the top of the tower it dripped from the tails like a sprinkling system, dousing the entire tower with water. But for all the protective covering of hides, earth, and so on, siege towers were still made of wood, and wood is vulnerable to fire.

At the siege of Acre in the Third Crusade, King Richard I of England reassembled several belfries previously made in Cyprus, including the great tower known as Malvoisin or "Bad Neighbor," which he renamed Malcousin or "Bad Relation." A Moslem account of the battle says the three towers, "each of sixty cubits in height," were so well protected that the defenders could not set them on fire. When the first efforts to burn their belfries failed, the Franks danced up and

This illustration, taken from a medieval manuscript, shows how innovative some siege-tower technology could be. Here, the roof of the tower rests on pivots, allowing it to be adjusted to deflect enemy fire while providing the optimum visual and firing range for the men on board.

down on top of the towers, jeering at the Saracens. But Greek fire finally proved effective, and all three towers went up in flames, giving the Franks, in the words of the Moslem author, "a taste of hell."

Once it began to burn, a belfry could quickly become a death trap, so extinguishing fires was an important job for the men on board. Some towers were fitted with buckets and cauldrons of water in anticipation of just such an event, but fighting fires often required the men to expose themselves to both the enemy and the flames as they climbed the tower to fight the blaze. Occasionally, fire would rush through one story after another so fast that no one in the tower had time to escape.

Although the equation has not often been

made, it seems likely that the development of the cannon signaled the end of the siege tower. The compact size, relative mobility, and destructive power of the cannon left the ungainly wooden towers with no effective defenses. At the siege of Malta in 1565, one of the belfries manned by the Turks was destroyed by novel means: a hole was secretly made in the wall of the Maltese castle, but the last stones on the outer face of the wall were left in place. When the tower had moved close to the wall, the final stones were pulled out to reveal the muzzle of a cannon. Loaded with chain shot, normally used to cut through ships' masts, one blast from the gun brought the tower and its inhabitants crashing to the ground.

For all of their unwieldiness, in the hands of a skilled engineer and a clever commander, a siege tower could be a surprisingly versatile weapon. The function of a tower could vary considerably to suit the needs of the moment. In addition to providing a bridge to reach the parapet wall, the fighting platform on top of the tower could be used to house mangonel and ballista, as well as crossbows and longbows. At the sieges of Tyre and Damietta, the crusaders' siege towers were fitted with a variety of stone-throwing engines.

The bottom level of the tower was also frequently adapted to house a battering ram. By the late Middle Ages, it often served as a cover for the activities of sappers busily chipping away at the castle wall, a tactic employed at the siege of Nicea. To conceal such clandestine operations, the lowest story of the belfry was sometimes fitted with a "penthouse," or roof jutting out at the front, to protect sappers or the head of a battering ram. In one of the more extreme examples of the possible uses for a siege tower, Richard the Lionheart dined in his while he was encamped at Messina on his way to the Holy Land.

Although engineers were responsible for the design and construction of belfries, the men who would actually man them were a group of knights, men-at-arms, and artillerymen. Archers primarily defended the belfries during their slow approach to the walls, while "gynours" (gunners) operated the various throwing engines that might be carried by the tower—such as the mangonel mounted on the roof of a tower employed during the Third Crusade. When it was finally time to storm the parapets, knights and men-at-arms replaced the archers on the upper levels. As the battle on the fighting platform and wall walks raged, the gynours moved to the lower level to operate the ram or sap the wall.

Jean de Froissart writes about the belfries used in 1345 at the siege of Reole, one of the earliest sieges of the Hundred Years' War.

Siege towers were sometimes used to house small artillery engines. When Henry III besieged Bedford Castle in 1217, he sent orders for "diversas machinas, patrarias, mangonillos, berefridum cum balistis"—that is, for a variety of engines, petraries, mangonels, and a belfry with a ballista. *The Dunstable Chronicle* speaks of the making of two towers higher than the tower of Bedford itself, and a sow for mining. As Matthew Paris claimed, Henry "spent much money before it was taken." No one but a king could have called on such a wide range of resources.

Thus the earl of Derby came before the town of Reole and laid siege thereto on all sides and made bastides [small fortresses] in the fields and on the ways, so that no provision could enter the town, and nigh every day there was an assault. The siege endured a long space. And then the month was expired that they of Segur should give up their town, the earl sent thither and they of the town gave up and became under the obeisance of the King of England.... The Englishmen that had made in the mean space two belfries of great timber with three stages, every belfry on four great wheels, and the sides towards the town were covered with cure-boly [cuir bouilli or toughened hides] to defend them from fire and from shot, and into every stage there was pointed an hundred archers. By strength of men these two belfries were brought to the walls of the town for they had so filled the dikes that they might be brought just to the walls. The archers in these stages shot so wholly together that none durst appear at their defense unless they were pavised [protected] by shields; and between these two belfries there were two hundred men with pickaxes to mine the walls, and so they brake through the walls.

Because siege towers had to be marginally mobile, there was a limit to how heavy, and therefore how solid, they could actually be. Written accounts confirm that they were not the most stable of structures. There are many stories of towers collapsing, killing scores of men in the process. At Verdun, a tower was tipped violently when the castles defenders snagged it with huge hooks and rocked it back and forth until the men inside fell out, only to be attacked and killed on the ground. At Odo I's siege of Montboyau, a huge belfry collapsed as a result of faulty construction, crushing everyone on board. When Odo finally abandoned the siege out of sheer frustration, the shattered tower was burnt in triumph by the citizens of Montboyau. A belfry used by the Swordbrothers in the Baltic region simply blew over in the gusty northern winds, and a tower at Nicaea was crushed and its entire compliment killed by the accumulated weight of rocks thrown onto the fighting platform from the castle walls. The fact that rocks could be thrown onto the top of the tower from the castle walls may indicate that the tower was too low to have been effective even if it had survived to reach its target.

For a siege tower to be effective, it had to be maneuvered as close as possible to the walls, and for all the ingenuity of wheels, pulleys, and causeways, mobility was always the belfries' greatest weakness. Bringing a tower within reach of a castle's walls usually meant getting it across a ditch or moat, and this required tipping masses of earth, turf, stones, wood, and bundles of sticks into the chasm to form a causeway solid enough, and level enough, to create a road capable of supporting the tower. This massive construction job had to be carried out under nearly continuous enemy fire. To protect the workers, sows were constructed around the work site. The men inside the sows slowly filled the ditch, pushing the shelter ahead of them. At Montreuil-Bellay in the 1150s, Geoffrey V of Anjou forcibly conscripted visitors to the nearby fair at Saumur, using them to help to fill the ditch. At the siege of Jerusalem during the crusades, Count Raymond and other noblemen offered to pay a penny for every three stones dropped into the ditch, and at Acre, a woman who was helping fill the ditch was severely wounded and, knowing herself to be dying, made a last request that her body be thrown into the ditch to help with the work.

The massive effort required to successfully move a tower to the wall of a castle was one of the most crucial aspects of many sieges.

Having pushed the tower into position, knights and men-at-arms once again prepare to battle the French.

board, and overnight it was protected by a force which included a hundred knights. Behind it came a smaller engine, a cat or penthouse, made of woven osiers, in which were young men from Ipswich, who had to keep it in position.

Siege towers lumbered from the attackers' camp to the walls of the castle on sets of wheels or rollers. Motive power could be supplied by men inside the tower, who would lever the wheels around with the help of crow bars; by men outside the tower, pushing it; or by oxen. If animal power was used, the beasts were usually fastened to traces running through pulleys staked near the castle walls; thus, the animals actually pulled away from the castle to move the belfry towards it.

Moving such cumbersome structures was an enormous and dangerous task even across level terrain. Only the most hardened fighting men undertook it. At the siege of Ma'arrat, the normally haughty knights even lent a hand to help move their tower into position. At Shrewsbury, when King Stephen constructed a belfry and aimed it against the gate rather then the wall, fires were lit, so that it could be pushed forward under cover of the smoke.

The terrain itself often proved an insurmountable challenge. At Laon, Hugh Capet employed a skilled engineer to build a tower, but the effort was wasted because no amount of tugging or heaving could move it up the steep approach to the castle. Not surprisingly, the

At Lisbon, during the Second Crusade, the progress of the tower is described in detail by the priest who probably made a sermon of dedication from on board the new structure.

It was moved forward ninety feet on the first day. On the second day it was moved on further, and also at right angles in order to approach the wall near the Porto do Ferro. There were archers and crossbowmen on

tower at Jerusalem could not operate up and down slopes either, for it was "always needing level ground if it were to be pulled along." At Damietta, the Franks chose a poor position for their tower, again being unable to approach the walls because of the steep incline.

Too often, after all the effort of construction and pushing, the towers would get stuck in wet ground. At Carlisle, for example, the ground was marshy, and men had to use ropes to haul out the engines. James of Aragon speaks of making a wooden track over which to move his tower. When completed, the track was greased to make the tower move quicker and smoother. This ingenious contraption was inched along by the type of ring and pulleys mechanism mentioned earlier. Despite the ingenious engineering involved in the project, it seems to have failed. James blamed his engineer for insisting the tower be moved before proper protective screens had been put in place, for when James and his men tried valiantly to haul the tower over the wooden causeway, it stuck halfway across. Enemy engines scored hits on the tower ten times during the lunch rest period and over a hundred times during the night. The tower finally had to be pulled back to safety.

The men, dozens or even hundreds of them engaged in moving the bulky structure forward inch by inch, were constantly open to attack from the walls. Towers inevitably became easy prey as they lumbered toward their target. At Dyrrachium (1108) and Damietta (1169), the defenders built their own towers inside the wall to directly counter those of the besiegers. Dyrrachium had built an earlier tower in 1081 and using mechanisms and manpower pushed a beam from it to jam shut the drawbridge of an attacking Frankish belfry. In 1111 the Moslem defenders of Tyre destroyed a Frankish siege tower by erecting their own tower fitted with an iron-sheathed

crane. The crane arm, fitted with a system of pulleys, allowed the defenders to winch buckets of flaming pitch across their parapet wall, then dump these down the side of the approaching tower. Sometimes defenders "softened up" the ground in front of a wall by digging pits and refilling them with loose earth, in the hope that if a siege tower was brought up it would sink into one of the pits and become immobile. Once stuck in one of these traps, a tower was useless and would probably have to be dismantled or abandoned.

With the tower at our fictional siege finally complete, the English are ready to mount their largest assault to date. The mine has been made ready to fire, and the English commander divides his forces into scaling

For many the siege tower became a death trap as missiles, ballista bolts, and Greek fire wreak havoc on the tower as it approaches the walls of the castle.

When the fire in the mine chamber burns away the support posts, the tower above wrenches itself away from the castle wall.

The collapsing tower creates a breach, allowing masses of English knights into the middle ward of the castle.

French soldiers rush from other points along the wall in a vain effort to fight back the English as they surge into the middle ward. Again, the skill and number of the English overpowers the French, and they are forced to retreat.

parties and troops to push and man the tower. Although his depleted forces are stretched to their limit, he must also keep enough men in reserve to rush the breach.

The French commander has been watching the progress of the tower that now stands only a few hundred yards from his walls. He is certain that the tower, along with a diversionary escalade, will be the Englishmen's last, best hope for overrunning his fortress, and he prepares the most devastating welcome he can devise, concentrating his defenses to face the tower.

As the completed tower creeps slowly toward the newly constructed causeway, English knights and men-at-arms begin another all-out escalade. By the time the tower reaches the causeway, flaming arrows have already started several small fires on its outer surface. A ballista mounted on a castle tower tears a hole in the side of the tower, blocking access to the staircase and impaling a man to the stair post as it crashes through the wall. Now, too close to the castle to retreat, the English have no option but to press forward.

As soon as the tower reaches the wall, the drawbridge is lowered onto the parapets and dozens of English knights wielding swords and axes pour into the castle to meet the defenders in glorious, bloody combat. As the battle on the wall rages, wafts of smoke escape from the foundations of the curtain wall on the opposite side of the castle.

With a thundering crash and the acrid stench of seared grease, a section of castle wall disappears in a cloud of dust and smoke. The moment the English see the wall topple, a wave of knights and men-at-arms surges through the breach. French soldiers frantically crawl through the debris in an attempt to drive them back, but the superiority of numbers is irresistible. The defenders are simply too few to repel the tripartite attack of the scalers on the walls, soldiers pouring through the breach, and the assault of the siege tower. The French commander and his men retreat in confusion to the keep and bar the entrance, but they are utterly demoralized. Desperately needed provisions, kept in a storehouse in the middle ward, are now in the hands of the English. The garrison's surrender, either through another such assault or by starvation, is now only a matter of weeks, or even days.

Chapter Ten

ENDGAME

Starvation Tactics

Having lost the middle ward to the English, the French have pulled back to the inner ward and the massive central keep. Though they are nearly without supplies, they are in a strong defensive position. Were the English to attempt another all-out assault against the inner wall or the keep itself, they would surely be repelled by the concentrated French forces. The English commander, aware of how daunting these two final obstacles are, will not attempt to storm the keep. This is one of those points in a siege where warfare exhibits all of the brinkmanship and patience of a game of chess. The English have discovered the storehouse of provisions. Cursory examination has shown that the stores were already being used (perhaps because other storehouses were destroyed by Greek fire). The French are now limited to whatever provisions are still in the cellars of the keep. The end, therefore, is only a matter of time. The English commander will simply blockade the tightly packed and poorly provisioned garrison in the hope of starving them out.

But to do so, the English Commander must keep his army in tact long enough for hunger to take its toll on the beleaguered.

There are various reasons why it is becoming ever more difficult for the English commander to keep his army together and under his control. This chapter, therefore, will examine various aspects of camp life both within and without the castle.

DISCIPLINE

" A nd when they had drunken enough of the wine that was in the taverns and other places, they full ungodly smote out the heads of the pipes and hogsheads of wine, that men went wet shod in wine, and then they robbed the town, and bare away bedding, cloth and other stuff, and befouled many women...." Thus reports an eyewitness on the Lancastrian army in Ludlow during the Wars of the Roses.

Normally a strict code of discipline was drawn up and published before a campaign, and enforced as much as possible during its course. Such codes were designed to protect the Church, women, and children from robbery and maltreatment. These codes sometimes specifically included prohibitions against assaults on all noncombatants and private property, and laid out prices to be paid for food, the treatment of prisoners, and the arrangements for disposal of booty.

The punishments for desertion, cowardice, and disobedience were also routinely spelled out; they were normally harsh and got harsher when conditions deteriorated—but medieval commanders could, on occasion, be more lenient than those of later centuries. Soldiers often enjoyed a measure of bargaining power, refusing to fight if not paid, demanding to air their grievances, and speaking up in support of accused comrades; it

The English commander, frustrated at his inability to overwhelm the fortress, decides that the best way to force the enemy to surrender is simply to wait and starve them out.

sometimes paid for a commander to tread lightly. We read of Charles the Bold addressing disgruntled English mercenaries in their own language, mixing flattery with threats. But when pushed too hard he would lash about him with his sword and order deserters put to death in a manner carefully calculated to discourage imitation.

Town levies (units of soldiers raised from a single town or city like those of Esslingen in 1476) were threatened with fines and banishment for any acts of insubordination or

When the English seized the middle ward of the castle, they gained control of one of the main French food stores. Now driven to the inner ward of the castle, the French are dangerously low on food.

This drawing, adapted from a medieval manuscript, depicts soldiers looting a town which they have over-run. Loot taken from defeated towns was an expected bonus for poorly paid soldiers and mercenaries.

cowardice. For a townsman, banishment meant loss of livelihood and protection: outside his town, he was an exile who belonged nowhere and might never be able to earn enough money to pay his fines and return home.

Such formal codes of behavior were, of course, enforced in accordance with the circumstances. Although individual wrongdoers might suffer their full rigor in a garrison or camp, assuming there was time to bother about such things, in more fluid circumstances, soldiers could often plunder and murder with impunity, as long as they did not openly defy their commander or fail disgracefully in their duty to him.

After a battle, soldiers frequently got completely out of hand; towns taken by assault were routinely given over to bouts of pillage and rape that could last for days at a time. In his *Chronicles*, Jean de Froissart recorded that "the land was undone and darkened with evil deeds, and men said openly that Christ and his angels slept." It was difficult to keep order, and commanders both inside castles and in charge of besieging forces realized that discipline was critical. Very often the question of law and order became a matter of trying to impose a moral order on an entire army. For example, when King Henry V of England invaded France in 1417, he stated that if any prostitutes were found in the army besieging Rouen, they would have their arms broken. Frequently, commanders laid down edicts that their soldiers shouldn't gamble, visit brothels, or swear.[35]

PROSTITUTES

As unusual as it might seem, when an army set off on campaign, they usually brought with them scores of prostitutes. It seems strange that medieval military commanders

Boredom was the soldier's biggest enemy during the weeks, or months, of a siege. Knights and commoners alike wile away the time gambling, drinking, and often quarreling, a disintegrating spiral of behavior that often led to the breakdown of order in the camp. The presence of prostitutes in camp helped relieve tension and provided a diversion for the soldiers.

would include "whores" on their packing list for a siege, but they certainly did. Prostitutes followed the army from place to place, from battle to battle and from country to country, serving a useful purpose and in general raising morale.

Most medieval armies were expected to have a large contingent of prostitutes following them; it was part of the routine services supplied. If an army failed, moralists often argued that it was because they had too many prostitutes with them and that the army did not,

therefore, have the right intentions in laying the siege.

Although the idea of a modern army marching off with a battalion of prostitutes in tow may seem somewhat incongruous, prostitution was viewed differently during the Middle Ages than it is today. Prostitutes were not catering merely to the lower classes, to the grunts, and the common soldiers. Knights, lords, and noblemen also made frequent and unashamed use of them. The omnipresence of prostitution; the surprisingly large number of prostitutes, especially in Rome, Naples, and Venice (where there were more than 11,000 in the sixteenth century); and the wealth and social success of certain prostitutes in Roman and Venetian high society in the fifteenth century all illustrate the success of the profession and the role played by prostitutes in breaching, however furtively, the barriers of polite society.

WOMEN IN SIEGE WARFARE

Women also played a very real part in the defenses of castles and towns; in desperate situations, they were well aware that they were fighting for their lives. There are many examples of arms and spare armor being issued to women. At the siege of Beauvais, France, in 1472, Burgundian attempts to take the town were abandoned after a twenty-five-day siege, a bombardment that demolished a quarter of the city walls, and several failed assaults. The town was saved by its determined garrison of men-at-arms, its townsmen, and its womenfolk. Inspired by Joan of Arc, Jeanne "Hachette" Laisne led a group of townswomen armed with axes in a sortie against the attackers. They drove the enemy from the town wall and captured the Burgundian standard, encouraging the Duke of Burgundy to abandon the siege. The women played such an important role in the battle that they were granted the right to wear whatever clothes they wished[36] and to precede their men in civic processions.

On the night of 19 July 1447, the German town of Soest was stormed, whereupon "the armed citizens hurried to man the walls, and the women started to boil water and pitch under the wall-walks and to prepare tubs of quicklime." The besiegers' scaling ladders turned out to be too short to reach the top of the walls, so "the defensive measures that the women had prepared, namely pitch and quicklime that could be poured on the attackers to inflict burns, were particularly effective."

Soldiers' wives, prostitutes, and other women accompanied medieval armies in sizable numbers. During the long weeks and months of the siege, the women tried to make camp life as pleasant as possible.

Enough similar descriptions survive to make it clear that women's participation in defense was the rule rather than the exception.

Large numbers of women also accompanied the armies, sometimes working in direct support of the military effort, sometimes actually fighting alongside the men. Some 4,000 women from a Burgundian encampment were once organized in an unsuccessful attempt to divert part of the Rhine. "These women," wrote an eyewitness, "were given a banner by the duke with a woman painted on it" and went to and fro "with banner, trumpets and pipes." There are examples of ladies of rank fighting fully armed in battle. In 1382 a woman was killed in battle in Flanders, bearing the Flemings' banner, and in 1396 a Fresian woman "dressed in blue like a madwoman" fell pierced by arrows during a battle between Fresia and Hainault.

We read, following a defeat of the Burgundian army, that during their retreat, "many women that were dressed in armour were struck down because they were unrecognized.... Many armed women, to protect their bodies and lives, exposed their breasts, proving that they were not men."

In a siege camp, there would be women for cooking and cleaning, for tending to the sick and wounded, for washing clothes and for picking lice out of the men's hair, not to mention the prostitutes (who would likely have been doing all of the other activities as well). Of course, the presence of large numbers of

If a siege looked like it was going to last for several months, the besiegers would often plant gardens, growing vegetables to supplement the food that could be obtained from local farmers and traders.

women in a siege camp could lead to problems of discipline. Under Charles the Bold's ordinances of 1473, no more than thirty women

In the fifteenth century, cards, bowls, ball games, board games, and many group games that would today be considered too simple for adults—though they were played rather more robustly in the Middle Ages than they are now—helped to pass the long days of boredom. Soldiers playing a rambunctious round of duck-duck-goose is not how we tend to picture the medieval military establishment, but it certainly did occur.

were allowed to travel with each company on campaign, and none of them as "private property"—even so, there was trouble. At the siege of Neuss in 1474, English soldiers quarreled over a wench and wanted to kill each other. The duke himself rushed to the spot to quell the trouble, but English archers "shot two or three times directly at him with their bows." The arrows passed close by the unarmored duke's head and shoulders, and his Burgundian soldiers, fearing assassination, rushed to attack the English mercenaries. The incident nearly caused a pitched battle in the camp.

We have very little specific information about the "tail" (women, boys, camp followers, and baggage) of medieval armies, but there is evidence that they were sometimes as large as those of the seventeenth century—which means they equaled the size of the army itself. There was less restriction on personal entourages in medieval times; in fact, they were an essential part of any nobleman's display of power and wealth. Valets, servants, cooks, musicians, priests, grooms, smiths, ferriers, carters, and all *their* countless helpers, boys, and women, could be present as part of the "official" establishment.

ACCOMMODATION

When a prince or duke went to war, he tried to take with him as much of the comfort and richness of his home as practical, in order to maintain his accustomed display of wealth and ceremony. Many-roomed tents of satin or brocade, thickly carpeted and hung with rich tapestries, would house the lord and his retinue. Both Charles the Bold and Henry VIII even took prefabricated wooden houses on campaign; Charles erected his between two great pavilions in which he took his meals and held council. The establishments of lesser lords and knights were relatively smaller and simpler, but they too had their retinues, for love of display extended throughout the propertied classes.

Duke Philip the Good's tent in the camp at Boulogne was a virtual portable palace and contained many dining rooms, bedrooms, and a chapel. It was reported to be

of extraordinary size, larger than ever seen before. The construction was so vast and elegant as to capture all eyes. It was a pavilion in the form of a town surrounded by wooden towers and crenelated walls. The entrance consisted of two great towers with a curtain [wall] suspended in between. In the middle of the tent was the main room, from which extended, like the spikes of a wheel, a large number of apartments separated by tiny alleys, in which it was said that 3,000 people could be lodged.

The fabric of the tents captured by the Swiss at Grandson was reportedly rich enough to be cut up for church vestments. Tents were decorated with identifying emblems, shields and flags, and appliqué strips of colored cloth, which also reinforced the seams, arranged to form simple geometric designs. Most officers and many soldiers were also provided with tents or housed in farms and villages. On the other hand, in Henry VIII's army it was forbidden to provide tents for the troops on the grounds that they took up too much space on the wagons and took too much time to put up and take down; nonetheless, many captains provided them for their men.

A contemporary account in the Lille archives describes tents for a Burgundian army. In January 1476 the army received "600 small tents and pavilions, 100 other square pavilions, two wooden houses, 130 square *tentelletes*, 50 other pavilions, six large tents and six square

Left: In the English camp, the brisk autumnal weather can pose a serious threat to morale and health.

Below: Although the knights are equipped with tents and pavilions befitting their social status, common soldiers and archers are left to their own devices, often sleeping on the bare ground, exposed to rain and cold.

pavilions and another wooden house." Tents and camp equipment were important to an army on the move and frequently ate up one-fifth of the expedition's total budget.

Those without tents were more or less adept at making shelters from hay, branches, or looted timber, and some probably carried canvas or blankets to make a "hale" or makeshift lean-to. In 1523 a Welsh soldier in France sneered at improvident campaigners: "And yet they had no reason to complain except of their own sluggishness and slovenliness. For there was no lack of food and drink or wood for fire and making huts, and plenty of straw to roof them and to lie on if they only fetched it, but there were many a man weak in body who preferred from sheer laziness to lie under the hedge rather than take the trouble to make a snug warm hut."

Siege camps were often enormous, laid out in streets, with hundreds of tents, markets, horse lines for thousands of animals, and an inner camp for the commanders. A site like this for 10,000 soldiers and their followers must have resembled a fair-sized town on a bustling market day, which is almost precisely how Jean de Froissart recalls the camp of Edward III at the siege of Calais:

> As soon as the King of England arrived before Calais, he began in earnest to make full preparations for a regular siege. Between the town, the river and the bridge... he had houses built of heavy planks, thatched with straw and brush wood and set out in properly ordered streets, as though they were to be lived in for a dozen years. He was determined to stay there through the winter and summer til Calais was his, without regard for the time and effort it might cost him. His new town had everything that an army could need and more, including a place to hold markets on Wednesdays and Saturdays.

> There were haberdashers and butchers' shops, stalls selling cloth and bread and all other necessities, so that almost anything could be bought there.... The King made no assaults on Calais, for he knew that the effort would be wasted. Desiring to spare his men and artillery, he said that he would starve the place out, however long it took....

Improbable as it sounds, siege camps often played host to local trade fairs. An army on the march or actively engaged in battle might well expect rations from its commanders, but at a siege, most of the soldiers were paid in coin and provided with some foodstuffs, depending on what was available. From their wages, soldiers were expected to supplement their diet by purchasing additional food and drink from local purveyors. Consequently, great markets often sprang up near encamped armies. At the siege of Neuss, a huge market was laid out within the confines of the Burgundian camp, with streets for stalls marked out with cords. Apothecaries, craftsmen, drapers, shoemakers, hatters, barbers, cutlers, and lantern and candle makers set up shop alongside grocers, butchers, fishmongers, and hay and oats suppliers. But such organization would be possible only when an army settled in for a prolonged siege.

RATIONS

We do not know how or when rations were issued to soldiers in camp, and customs probably varied widely. It appears that soldiers were issued their basic rations and made their own arrangements for cooking, just as they continued to do until the late nineteenth century. Some documents speak of soldiers having to buy rations out of their pay.

The system of supply and the financial

structure which supported it were fragile and quickly broke down in the face of setbacks. A lost battle, a prolonged siege, a missed rendezvous, promised supplies withheld—if any of these occurred, then hunger joined disease and violent death to stalk the troops. Hungry soldiers were unscrupulous even in their own country, and the many mercenaries in fourteenth and fifteenth century armies lacked even the vague inhibition of peer pressure inspired by common nationality.

The arrival of a large, hungry army—even a "friendly" one—in a rural area could cause a disaster of biblical proportions. If the army took the winter store of harvested crops and seed grain, ran off the few cattle kept alive for the spring, stole tools and carts, tore apart fences and outbuildings for firewood, then winter brought famine to whole communities. Famine was often the catalyst for violent population shifts: Peasants who did not starve fled to the nearest towns; on their heels came disease and the breakdown of order. The terror caused by plundering armies is one of the most ancient and universal side effects of warfare.

As discussed in chapter 4, the defenders would often employ a scorched-earth policy before the arrival of the besiegers, making matters even worse. When a long-term supply of adequate provisions was essential for the attacking army's campaign, the scorched-earth policy was severely felt. There are numerous examples of this policy at work. At Dunster, England's King Stephen left nothing at all "that could serve his enemies for food or any purpose." At Le Mans, Helias made things difficult for the attackers by taking into the castle everything that could be gathered and destroying the rest, "so that the cruel raiders could find nothing." One raiding army of Scots was advised not to leave behind even a meal for the next day, not so much as an ox for the plough; and at Belford they set fire to the farms, took clothes, oxen, horses, cows, ewes, and lambs, as well as money and valuables. Rahewin describes in detail the destruction done around Milan, where vineyards were flattened and fig and olive groves destroyed so that famine and disease inevitably followed.

The scorched-earth tactic was intended to deprive the besieging army of desperately needed supplies and provisions, forcing it to rely on prior preparation or keep the siege short. When food or water ran low and a besieging force was under orders to maintain the siege, the ensuing famine could prove horrendous.

Contemporary manuals mention ideal quantities for rations, which are corroborated by the financial accounts of actual deliveries. We can draw up a list of a "typical" day's rations for a well-fed fourteenth- or fifteenth-century soldier: 2–3 lbs. of bread, a "pfund" or 1 lb. of fresh meat, $\frac{1}{4}$ oz. each of salt pork and eggs, and $\frac{1}{2}$ oz. each of cheese and butter. This totals about 4,300 to 4,500 calories a day, sufficient for hard physical work in the open air. To this might be added vegetables or fruit as available. The basics—bread or biscuits, salt pork or beef, beans, and cheese—would be familiar to any soldier down the centuries. As always, when the food was issued in reasonable condition, it came to the table as good or bad as the cooks.

FOOD SHORTAGES

In late October 1097, crusaders besieged the great fortified city of Antioch, which was well provisioned and ably defended by the Seljuk emir Yagi Siyan. As the siege dragged on (it lasted nine months) and winter came, the Christian army suffered in such extreme that desertions were frequent; many died of famine, many others of disease and exhaustion. The crusaders' ranks were thinned to an alarming degree. The *Gesta Francorum* records that the crusaders were "forced to eat carrion and leaves, thistles which pricked the tongue, dried horse-skin, and seeds of grain found in manure." When food was available to be purchased, prices were extortionate: "Wine cost too much even to mention, a tongueless

Balancing food supplies to the number of men in a garrison, and to the longest possible time that a siege may last, was integral to allowing a garrison to hold out until a relief force arrived.

As provisions dwindle, food becomes more valuable than money. Here, French soldiers gamble for possession of a few plums.

horse's head was two or three shillings, and a goat's intestines five shillings; a hen cost fifteen shillings, an egg two shillings, and a walnut a penny." Unable to obtain any other kind of food, the humbler crusaders turned to cannibalism, making the most of any Saracens they killed. The horses suffered equally with their owners, and in a few months the total number of mounts was reduced from more than 70,000 to a mere 2,000. Unusually heavy rains turned the whole camp into a morass; tents rotted and decayed in the wet, and, it was said, the camp soon presented the appearance of a vast graveyard.

Of the siege of Acre (1189–91) the *Itinerarium* records that:

Meanwhile the food shortage came to a crisis; the middle-rank troops as well as the lower were tormented by hunger, which as it grew, became not just severe but unremitting. The situation was aggravated by worsening feelings about the provocative behavior of the marquis, Conrad of Montferrat, who was secretly passing food supplies only to those who were allies and accomplices of his wicked designs [on the throne of Jerusalem].

...What more can be said? A measure of wheat small enough to tuck under your arm was selling for a hundred pieces of gold, a fowl for 12 shillings and an egg for six pence....

At another siege when the garrison ran short of provisions, the commander (in this instance Roger de Lacy) "mustered separately those men who were capable of fighting. For these he reckoned the food he had would amount to a year's supply." The rest, 1,200 of them, were sent out of the castle. "He had no doubt he was sending the wretches to their deaths, nor did he care what fate overtook them provided he could save the fort for a short time. The rabble (as Le Breton describes them) streamed out like a flight of bees. Soon their joy changed to sorrow, for the French drove them back with spears and javelins. They rushed back to the gates only to find them shut and barred. Cannibalism broke out, and a bird which fell among them was eaten feathers, feet, and all. Dogs and rats stood no chance whatever. The unfortunate men who were pinned between besiegers and besieged hung grimly onto life until Philip Augustus inspected the forward lines. When they saw him, they begged for bread and mercy, both of which they received. It was obvious that they were too weak to do either good or harm to anyone. Scenes such as these were a far too common occurrence in medieval sieges.

SIEGE OF CALAIS

One of the most notorious starvation sieges took place when Edward III of England mounted a year-long siege against Calais in 1346. Despite the fact that Calais was one of the most well-defended cities in France, surrounded by defensive ditches and open marshland and supporting a large garrison of soldiers, Edward managed to blockade the port with 700 English man-of-war ships and completely surrounded the town with English troops. He then built the aforementioned siege town—with shops, taverns, and barracks to keep his men comfortable—and calmly waited for the town to capitulate.

John of Vienne, governor of Calais, sent away nearly 2,000 nonessential citizens of the city to make the food supplies last as long as possible. King Edward, in an act of generosity, not only allowed the ejected citizenry to pass unharmed through his lines, but he gave them all a hot meal and a small amount of money to help them on their way. Several months later, when the governor attempted to send out another group of 500, the King was in no mood for generosity. The English refused to let them pass, and the French refused to let them back inside the city. Trapped between these two opposing camps, 500 once brave men and women were allowed to starve to death huddled against the walls of their town.

Even an army sent by the king of France to relieve the city could not raze the siege and were driven back after only a few weeks. Calais could not be rescued. When the city raised the English flag as a sign of surrender on 4 August 1347, the only lives that had been lost were those of the 500 French who had been condemned to a slow starvation death by their own governor.

With the city's food supply gone, the

Drawn from a period manuscript, this illustration shows the six leading burghers of Calais surrendering the keys to England's Edward III when he successfully brought their city to its knees.

WATER SHORTAGES

Baldwin de Redvers, who rebelled against King Stephen of England, must be one of the unluckiest men in history. Baldwin first rebelled at Exeter, but the unusually hot summer of 1138 caused the water supply to dry up and he was forced to accept terms. He then went on to the Isle of Wight and defied the king again from behind the walls of Carisbrooke Castle, but once more the well dried up and he had to flee, leaving the garrison of the castle to surrender to the king.

A lack of water forced de Redvers to capitulate and accept terms for surrender, but in some instances, withdrawal was not so easy. In the Holy Land, the Saracen warlord Saladin adopted a variation on the scorched-earth tactic by poisoning wells as he and his army retreated from Arsouf to the capital city of Jerusalem. When the crusaders besieged Jerusalem in 1099, the *Gesta Francorum* records:

During the siege we were so oppressed by thirst that we sewed together the bodies of oxen and buffalo, which we used to carry water over a distance of about six miles. Because of the vile-smelling water from these vessels and the barley bread, we were in daily distress and affliction, for the Saracens used to lie in wait around the springs and water sources, and would ambush our men, kill them and cut them to pieces, and would also lead off our animals into their own caves and hideouts. We were so distressed by thirst that even for one penny a single man could not buy enough water to quench his thirst.

governor asked Edward for the lives and liberties of the citizens as the sole condition of surrender, but Edward, incensed at their obstinate resistance, was determined to punish them all. However, when his officers appealed to his chivalry, he softened his resolve and he compromised his anger by demanding that six of the leading citizens should be sacrificed instead of the whole populace. These ill-fated six should come to his camp in their shirts, bareheaded and barefooted, with halters round their necks, and bearing the keys of the city. Six prominent citizens volunteered their lives to save the others and went to Edward in the condition he had demanded. The king ordered them to be instantly executed, but his queen begged for their lives and he could not refuse her.

A lack of food could end a siege before it began, or break a stalemate in a drawn-out conflict, but a lack of clean drinking water, as we have mentioned, could be even worse.

As the siege went on, the shortage of water became so acute that the soldiers sought relief by any available means, drinking their horses' blood, each other's urine, and even burying themselves in damp sand in the hopes of absorbing moisture through their skin.

In the twelfth century, the German Emperor Frederick Barbarossa gained entry to one Italian city by putting corpses into the stream running into the city, thereby polluting the town water supply. Often sulfur was dumped into streams to make the water inside the city or castle undrinkable. These tactics, while often successful, were widely regarded as vaguely unchivalrous and would normally be attempted only once all other methods of attack had been tried without success.

In an attempt to prevent such horrific scenes of suffering, both sides agreed to a given date whereby the siege would either have

Disease, infection, and starvation eventually took their toll on both sides in a siege. The elderly and those already weakened by wounds were particularly vulnerable to the effects of poor nourishment and exposure.

More devastating than a shortage of food is a lack of clean water. When the drinking water becomes polluted or, as we see here, the well runs low and the water becomes brackish, it can force an army to surrender within a few days.

to be accomplished or relieved. This date would be set at the onset of a siege, during the negotiation stage (see chapter 5). The predetermined date for capitulation, conquest, or surrender was an effective and necessary precaution against the diminishing of supplies for both the besiegers and the besieged. By establishing such a date, neither side should have to face such an ignominious and unchivalrous fate as starving to death.

Matthew Paris recorded that Roger, earl of Winchester, came under siege at Galwey during the reign of England's King Henry III. Roger was taken by surprise and without sufficient provisions to withstand a siege. He decided that he would rather die an honourable death in battle than starve to death and chose to make a desperate sortie against considerable odds. Remarkably, the sortie worked and his enemies fled allowing Roger to escape.

The whole picture of what is at work

In conference with their commander, the French officers and knights urge him to surrender. The commander stands firm, insisting that the King will send a relief force before they are forced to capitulate to the English.

to provision them and their horses. No grass could grow, nor any other eatable thing, so hard and dry and sunbaked was the earth. Anything that did come up withered quickly because of the excessive summer heat. To get supplies, the English had to send their servants and foragers anything up to sixty miles before they found them....

When they rode about the district... and saw from a height or distance what looked like a large village, they were glad and went towards it in the hope of finding provisions and booty. But when they got there they found only walls and ruined houses, with not a dog or a cat or a cock or a hen or a man or woman among them. Everything had been wrecked and despoiled by the French themselves. So their effort and time were wasted and they went back to their commanders having accomplished nothing. Their horses were lean and weak for lack of proper food, and fortunate indeed when they found grass to eat. They could hardly be ridden, having become so sickly that they died on the road of heat and exhaustion. Like them, some of the greatest lords were desperately ill with fevers and shivering-fits.

The morning chill struck through their whole bodies, giving them sickness and fever and afflicting them with dysentery,[37] of which they inevitably died. It was the same with barons, knights and squires as with humble people.

here, from the scorched-earth policy to the shortage of food or water to the eventual and inevitable onset of disease, may be glimpsed by Jean de Froissart's account of John of Gaunt's expedition to Spain. Froissart writes:

Their men were quartered in the country, where there was a great scarcity of everything

Camp conditions were certainly a cause of many failed sieges, usually from illness and death, with the attendant loss of manpower and morale. At Cologne the chronicler describes the "stench of the camp," which as he remarks "is usually the case." Illness, brought on by poor food and difficult conditions, was indeed a common fear for both besiegers and besieged. Le Sap was one of many places where destruction led to shortages as flocks and herds were killed. The Angevin attackers had meat, but not fires or salt. They were clearly so ravenous that they ate the meat raw, without salt or bread. It seems they were short of bakers and cooks. As a result of this, says the chronicler: "By God's judgment almost all suffered from dysentery; plagued by diarrhea, they left a trail of filth behind and many were barely capable of dragging themselves back home."

Our English commander, having decided to starve out the French defenders, feels certain that he can maintain order and discipline among his troops long enough for time, hunger, and disease to take its toll on the besieged garrison. Unbeknownst to him, however, a massive French relief force has set off to break the siege and engage the invading English in the open field.

Chapter Eleven

THE BIG BANG

Gunpowder and Cannons

During the latter Middle Ages, one weapon, which has not been mentioned in our fictitious siege, made increasing appearances on the battlefield. That weapon was gunpowder. One cannot, it would seem, discuss castles without eventually addressing the topic of gunpowder. As a relatively small detachment of a much larger army, the besieging English at our fictional siege would be unlikely to have cannons. If there are guns in the English arsenal, which is certainly possible in the late fourteenth century, they would travel with the main army. The French relief force, on the other hand, are hauling a number of cannons and bombards through the countryside to greet their unwelcomed visitors. From the high Middle Ages onward, gunpowder and the weapons associated with it slowly worked their way onto the field of battle and, in the process, changed the siege, castles, the composition of armies, and the nature of warfare itself.

We know surprisingly little about the actual origins of gunpowder, probably because the people who carried out the earliest experiments in explosives were aware of its potential danger. The compound itself was dangerous and so was the possibility of religious and political fallout from delving into such mysterious areas. Consequently, scientists and scholars destroyed the evidence of their work or disguised it in coded manuscripts.

As early as the tenth century, the Chinese probably developed some form of explosives with essentially the same component parts as gunpowder (charcoal, saltpeter, and sulfur), which they used for firing rockets and—it is vaguely possible—some form of cannon. The near legendary tale of Marco Polo returning from China carrying the magical powder in 1295 may be true, but the fact is that gunpowder had made its appearance in Europe well before Polo's time. European monks first uncovered tantalizing bits of information about gunpowder from Moorish alchemists in Spain shortly after 1200. The most famous early dabbler in the explosive arts was the English scholar Roger Bacon, who, in turn, was introduced to the subject by his teacher Albertus Magnus.

In the 1240s, Albertus Magnus came across, and copied, portions of a book entitled *Liber Igneum* (Book of Fire), probably written around 1200 by one of the monks who had visited Moorish Spain. Certainly Magnus shared this information with Roger Bacon, but whether Bacon was already working on explosives at this time is unknown. Whatever the case, Bacon was aware of the personal danger inherent in his work. Consequently, the surviving notes and records of his experiments of 1249 are written in cryptically coded language. But no amount of camouflage could keep scholars throughout Europe from finding out about such experiments and building on each other's work.

Nearly half a century elapsed between the creation of the first functional gunpowder and the invention of the cannon. During this period, kegs of gunpowder were adopted by miners, who found them far more effective tools for bringing down sections of wall and towers than brushwood and hog carcasses. The first recorded use of gunpowder by miners was at an English siege carried out against the Scots at Sterling Castle in 1304. That same year it was used in a field battle at Brechin in much the same manner land mines are used today.

The development of the cannon—even more than the origins of gunpowder—is lost in obscurity. For centuries experiments had been carried out whereby rockets and projectiles were launched from tubes, using Greek fire as a propellant. Unfortunately Greek fire has almost no explosive force, and the experiments were a failure. At some point shortly after 1300, gunpowder was substituted for other propellants and history's first gun actually fired. To make the origins of the gun even more confusing, early cannon and siege engines were often described by chroniclers with nearly identical phrases.[38] There is an account of Henry III "making daily assaults when guns and other ordnance were shot into the city." But because this account dates from less than twenty years after Roger Bacons experiments, it must either be a description of a siege engine or an inaccurate later translation.

The first reliable account of a cannon's existence comes from a single matter-of-fact entry on an armament inventory from Ghent (now in Belgium) taken in 1313. Buried among hundreds of other items, one line simply notes the existence of "bussen met kruyt" (cannon with powder). This may have been the same gun that saw action at the siege of Metz in 1326, the same year the first cannons were cast for the city of Florence. The year 1326 also

The earliest known illustration of a gun shows a short-barreled field piece with a massive breach and a bore probably no more than two inches in diameter. The immense breech clearly shows that experiments had already proven the need for extra mass at the rear of a gun, where the explosion actually occurred. The projectile protruding from the muzzle seems to be an arrow, indicating that this was an antipersonnel or anticavalry weapon. We assume that the arrow was wrapped in leather to fill the bore. Gun arrows, similar to those fired by ballista, would have weighed between fifteen and thirty pounds, and although arrows were quickly replaced by stone balls and small iron shot, there are instances of arrows still being used as late as the siege of Ardres in 1377. Because the gun shown in this illustration lacks any form of carriage, it would have been impossible to guarantee its aim.

Walter de Milemete's illuminated manuscript of 1327 showing a bulbous cannon laying on a table and loaded with a large arrow gives our first glimpse of the future of medieval warfare.

gave us the earliest known visual depiction of the new weapon. Tucked in the bottom corner of an illuminated manuscript, a man can clearly be seen firing a primitive cannon. Fourteen years later, in 1340, we find a rather quaint account of a payment to French arms merchant Jehan Piet de Fur, for the purchase of "three tubes of thunder."

Early guns were usually made in bell foundries, where the technology of casting large quantities of bronze, without the finished product splitting as it cooled, was already well established. Because they were the acknowledged masters of metal working, bell founders often hired themselves out as gunners, implying that the secrets of metallurgy were some-

how integral to the loading and firing of cannon. The concept of specialist gun crews must have caught on immediately, because as early as 1326 an Italian legal document briefly mentions a "maestro delle bombarde" or master of the siege gun.

Although they brought a lot of noise and confusion to the battle field, the earliest cannon were so inaccurate that they were only an incidental danger to enemy soldiers. Lacking any form of carriage, guns were either strapped to a table or board, or simply propped against a mound of earth, making them impossible to aim and likely to shift when fired. As unreliable as the guns themselves was the powder used to fire them. The ingredients were carried separately and mixed together just before loading into the gun. This not only slowed the rate of fire but was likely to cause spontaneous ignition in the mixing ladle. Experiments with early gunpowder formulas show that at least a quarter of the shots would have misfired or failed to ignite entirely.

Despite their relative ineffectiveness, gunners were even more despised by the warrior nobility than the common rabble who made up the ranks of the army, including the engineers and miners. The unspeakable machines they operated brought an unbearable noise, clouds of smoke, and the hellish stench of burning

From Vannoccio Biringuccio's Pirotechnia, previously cited as the source for the Greek fire recipe, comes these instructions for making gunpowder:

Three [components] are the foundation of all, namely saltpeter [potassium nitrate], sulfur and charcoal. It is also necessary to make powder in accord with the effects of the engines that it is to be used in, because heavy guns do not require the same kind as small ones....

Now in order to make common powder for heavy guns, take three parts of refined saltpeter, two of charcoal made from willow wood, and one of sulfur. Everything is incorporated well together by grinding finely by ecorning [a process where the gunpowder was rolled with a cloth and sifted through a sheet of parchment which had been punched with holes of a desired size] and then dried of all moisture.

But since these powders are things that ignite very easily when they are being made, they would not be without danger to the one who makes them if he did not prevent this by moistening. Therefore, take care not to crush them while dry. Moisten it with ordinary water so that it sticks together when squeezed in the hand.

In order to compound it, the best and quickest method, take the quantity of saltpeter that you wish to put in the work and put it in a kettle with as much water as will suffice to dissolve it and put it on the fire to heat. After it is dissolved, remove it [from the fire] and measure out the suitable quantity of charcoal and by stirring mix it with the dissolved saltpeter. Throw your finely ground sulfur on top while you stir the charcoal with a stick, as is done with cheese and macaroni [the author's exact words]. By stirring it continually proceed to mix it. Then put the composition to dry out somewhat. To make it fine and incorporate it you have only to crush the charcoal and diligently dry it of every trace of moisture and then sift it very well with a fine sieve. Then, moistening it again with ordinary water or some vinegar, force it through a sieve to granulate it. Dry it out again and put it in dry wooden vessels to keep it.

The very nature of the siege changed with the introduction of gunpowder. By the end of the Hundred Years' War the increasing use of gunpowder was turning the battlefield into a nightmare of smoke, fumes, and noise.

sulfur to the battlefield. Little wonder gunners were widely believed to be necromancers in league with the devil.

Those who were captured were likely to have their head shoved down the barrel of their gun, just before it was touched off. Considering the large number of gunners who were convicted criminals released from prison only to be chained to a gun, after minimal instruction, and promised that if the gun did not explode (or they were not captured and murdered by the enemy), they would be released at the end of the battle, the early artillery corps was hardly a job with much of a

future. When the Bolognese army fielded a unit of handgunners against Venetian mercenaries in 1439, they nearly won the battle. Furious at mounted knights being blown off their horses by gunners, the victorious Venetians slaughtered all of their Bolognese prisoners for the cowardly use of such infernal weapons.

Although their effectiveness was more luck than skill, early cannons did produce two major changes in warfare. For the first time, there was a weapon requiring so much money and advanced technology to produce that its ownership was restricted to kings and great princes. Secondly, the appearance of gunpowder-fired weapons was almost simultaneous with the development of fully articulated plate armor, the perfection of the armorer's art. Each development greatly increased the demand for the other, one as an offensive weapon, the other defensive. The effectiveness of good armor as a defense against hand cannon can be seen in the story of Don Francisco de Senoguera who, during the siege of Malta, survived a direct hit in the chest from a musket ball. A later shot, which hit him in the unarmored groin, however, killed him.

EARLY USE OF CANNONS

At the cutting edge of military technology since their adoption of the longbow, the English were quick to make the most of the cannon. Edward II took half a dozen field pieces along on his 1346 French campaign that culminated in the battle of Crécy. By positioning the guns at the flanks of his foot soldiers' units, Edward limited them to a support capacity, but considering the limited effectiveness of cannons at this time, this decision may have been most reasonable. In his chronicle of the battle of Crécy, Froissart notes that the English had guns "producing a great noise and throwing little stones to frighten the horses." Did this mean that the guns were firing grapeshot, or that each gun fired numerous, small caliber, single-shot rounds? We may never know, but in either case, it was apparently the first time the French had encountered the cannon, and the effect was dramatic. Although the heroes of the day were certainly the English longbowmen, the noise, smoke, and confusion of the guns must have added tremendously to what is certainly one of history's greatest routs.[39]

Despite their shortcomings, early cannons were almost immediately incorporated into siege technology. By the late 1300s, accounts speak of siege guns being brought to bear on the walls of castles and fortified towns alike. But early siege guns were so massive and cumbersome that they could not possibly keep up with armies on the march, often arriving at a siege weeks after camp had been established, when the battle was in full swing. The siege gun owned by the city of Nurenburg weighed 6,000 pounds and transporting it required twelve horses. The base on which it rested was even larger, requiring sixteen horses, while the service train carrying shot, powder, and equipment needed another nine wagons, each pulled by two to four horses.

But these huge guns, frequently referred to as bombards, did not immediately replace more traditional siege engines like the trebuchet and mangonel; they were simply integrated into the arsenal along with the other weapons and brought into use wherever they could do the most damage.

In regard to the siege of Romorantin in 1356, Froissart recorded:

Some of the wiser [English] men-at-arms reflected that they were striving in vain [against the castle] and letting their men be killed and wounded to no purpose, since they would never take the castle just by shooting arrows and hurling stones. They therefore ordered cannon to be brought forward to shoot bolts and Greek fire into the courtyard. If the fire caught there, it might well spread to the roofs of the castle towers, which were thatched with straw at that time....
Accordingly, fire material was brought up and shot from bombards and cannon and spread so rapidly that everything began to burn.

From this we get a clear idea that somehow, flaming Greek fire was shot from the cannon as a form of "bomb" intended to do more widespread damage than could possibly be accomplished by a single stone ball.

Lacking an effective carriage, early cannons were mounted on a simple wooden horse. Although unreliable, slow to load, and dangerous to operate, the cannon's potential as a weapon quickly made it an indispensable aspect of warfare.

The same year as Romorantin, the English found themselves besieged by the French at Breteuil, and again used their cannon to great effect against their enemy. Froissart wrote:

> The [English] garrison had seen a siege tower being built and formed a fairly clear idea of the French plan of attack. They had accordingly equipped themselves with cannons casting fire and big, heavy bolts of great destructive power. They made ready to assault the tower and defend themselves with great spirit. First, before using their cannon they engaged in open combat with the men in the tower.... When they had had enough of this, they began to fire their cannon and fling fire on top of the tower and inside it, and

with heavy volleys of their big bolts, by which many of the besiegers were killed and wounded and others so harassed they did not know which way to turn.

Curiously, it seems that rather than simply relying on the guns to destroy the siege tower and the men inside it, the English knights demanded a few hours of chivalric "play time," engaging in hand-to-hand combat before getting serious enough about winning the battle to bring their guns into the action.

During the era of traditional siege technology, the taller a castle's walls, the more unassailable they were. With the development of cannon, the reverse became true. High walls were not only an easier target, the avalanche of falling stone, collapsing walls, and timber made them as much a death trap as a sanctuary. When it was the outer curtain walls that were the target of cannon, the cascades of crumbling masonry often fell into the moat or dry ditch, forming a causeway leading directly to the developing breach in the wall. Certainly the "petard," a gun designed to be bolted directly to the face of a castle door with the intent of tearing the door from its hinges (thus filling the passageway with a shower of exploding wood and shrapnel) was a vast improvement over the time-consuming and dangerous tactic of ramming. Where an arrow shot into a castle gate had once signaled the official beginning of a siege, a cannonball now carried the same message—often taking the entire door along with it.

The first known instance of a cannon being powerful enough to effectively breach castle walls took place in 1377 when the duke of Burgundy's guns opened a hole in the castle wall at the siege of Odruik. Thirty years later, chroniclers and soldiers alike were claiming that no wall could withstand a concentrated assault of gunfire. By the end of the fourteenth century, every major power, and any power aspiring to be a major player, had an arsenal stocked with gunpowder-fired weapons. Between 1382 and 1388, a single gun maker supplied the English crown with seventy-three cannons; even the pope's army was stockpiling siege guns. Just as longbowmen had driven the mounted knight from his position of prominence on the battlefield, so the handgun was set to replace the archer. The cannon would soon outclass the siege engine.

Still, at the dawn of the fifteenth century, castles held their ability to allow a very few people to successfully defend a stronghold against a vastly superior force. Christine de Pisan, who compiled a list of supplies needed to withstand a siege (found earlier in this book), figured that a walled town of average size needed only twelve cannons to successfully

In the age of the cannon, as had been true of siege warfare from the beginning, the work of reducing the castle is carried out largely by commoners, while knights stand idly by waiting for their chance to win honor and glory.

This photo shows how traditional arrow loops were adapted to accommodate cannons. By placing the circular opening higher in the loop, hand cannons could be fired through the same opening.

cannon and hand cannon were simply integrated into existing castle defenses. Arrow loops were widened at the height of a cannon muzzle, or gun ports were cut into exterior walls just above ground level to allow the guns to sweep through the ranks of an approaching enemy. Along the parapets, guns were mounted on platforms and towers. The already well-defended barbican gate was enhanced by the addition of bulwarks (bastilles in French), which were hillocks of dirt designed to serve as emplacements for batteries of cannons. But the confined nature of castles proved as big a hindrance as an advantage for the use of the cannon. Maneuvering the cumbersome weapons on the confined walkways of a parapet wall was almost impossible, and the narrow spaces between wards made moving them from place to place equally difficult. Nonetheless, cannons became so inextricably linked with the siege that even when they were used in open battle, traditional siege tactics were usually employed. Temporary ditches were dug to form breastworks from which the guns could be fired in relative safety. This practice was so common that both sides often employed the same tactic, effectively immobilizing both armies while either, or both, could just as easily have maneuvered their guns to take advantage of the terrain and weaknesses in the opposition's lines.

When Henry V invaded France in 1415, along with his siege towers, ram heads, sows, scaling ladders, ballista, and trebuchet, he took a number of cannons from his armories at Bristol and the Tower of London, plus sixty-five gunners to man them. Although he is best remembered for his successes in the deployment of his longbowmen against the French,

defend itself, while a besieging force would need more than ten times as many guns to overwhelm the same town.

CASTLE DEFENSES AND SIEGE GUNS

Although guns were considered more effective in the siege than in field battles, they were not numerous enough, nor threatening enough, to require the construction of fortifications specifically to accommodate them. The

Henry was also a master strategist in the use of the cannon. At the siege of Harfleur, he bombarded the town so effectively that he not only opened several breaches in the city walls but also destroyed houses and buildings throughout the town. Although they made every effort to repair the breaches, the more than 10,000 stones fired into the town proved more than the French could withstand. In addition to the number of rounds fired in the bombardment, Henry's secret lay in the sheer size of his guns. Once again the English had introduced a new element into warfare: the monster culvern and the siege mortar.

The culvern, an oversized siege cannon designed specifically for long-term emplacement at sieges, was a technological breakthrough. Bell bronze could not be cast in the quantities required to make culverns and mortars without cracking as it cooled. Equally significant, the new consolidated gunpowder that was beginning to appear produced a much greater explosion and more stress on the gun barrel. An entirely new approach to manufacturing cannons had to be found. Gunsmithing was transferred to blacksmiths, who devised a method of forging without casting. Long, flat metal bars were arranged horizontally around an open core, like the staves of a barrel. Then a second (and sometimes a third) layer of straps was laid on top of the first to build up the thickness of the walls and cover the seams between the bars. The completed tube was held together with a series of closely spaced lateral bands, like barrel hoops, serving much the same purpose: to keep the staves securely together when the barrel was put under pressure. In all probability, the similarity between a stave-and-hoop culvern and a wine cask was the reason why the business end of a gun became known as the "barrel." As dubious as the process sounds, it seems to have worked. One of the

earliest guns of this design was made in 1375 for the king of France. Its construction required four master smiths, eight assistants, 2,300 pounds of iron, and occupied the entire market place of the city of Caen. Two years later the duke of Burgundy owned a similar gun, powerful enough to fire a stone ball weighing 200 pounds, and was in the process of ordering another one twice as large.

Monster culverns and giant bombards were enormous by any standards. The Mons Meg, cast for Philip of Burgundy in 1449, weighed 15,366 pounds without its carriage, and the Mad Margot (also known as Mad Margaret) weighed in at more than 36,145 pounds and fired a ball weighing 1,300 pounds. The actual sizes of some of these guns can best be judged by the number of horses required to move them.

Here we see a manuscript illumination of an early carriage-mounted gun being used in a siege around 1450.

In France in 1470, Louis XI's culvern required forty-one horses to pull it. We might think that such behemoth weapons would be unbelievably slow to fire and reload, but surprisingly the crew of the Mons Meg once managed to discharge her twenty-four times in only two and one half hours—a firing rate of once every six and one-half minutes.

Such huge weapons, with such impressive rates of fire, demanded hundreds of wagons laden with shot and powder to service them. In the campaign season of 1425–26, Henry VI's army went through 12,000 pounds of powder. Fifty years later the city of Milan routinely stockpiled 190,000 pounds of powder in its arsenal.

Guns requiring such massive quantities of powder and shot must have demanded an incredible amount of skill and teamwork to handle effectively. An account of Burgundian gunners at the battle of Bourge in 1411 shows great admiration for the skill of the engineers:

It shot stones of enormous weight at the cost of quantities of gunpowder and much hard and dangerous work on the part of the expert crew. Nearly twenty men were required to handle it. When it was fired, the thunderous noise could be heard four miles away, and terrorized the local inhabitants as if it were some reverberation from hell. On the first day, the foundations of one of the towers were partly demolished by a direct hit. On the next day this cannon fired twelve stones, two of which penetrated the tower, thus exposing many of the buildings and their inhabitants.

Half a century later, in 1466, Charles the Bold of Burgundy besieged the city of Dinant, bombarding it for eight months and destroying it so completely that the few surviving inhabitants were reduced to living in bombed-out cellars.

Impressive as it was, the monster gun was always the exception. Most guns, whether for field battle or the siege, were well within a more manageable range of sizes. The smaller and more maneuverable a gun was, however, the less likely it was to be of much use beyond spreading purely random terror. But sometimes random terror is enough. At the siege of Meaux in 1422, the son of Sir John Cornwall, a close friend of Henry V, was beheaded by a cannon-ball. At the siege of Orléans six years later, the earl of Salisbury climbed into a tower far beyond the city walls to reconnoiter the situation inside the town. When the French targeted the tower, the earl saw the first shot coming and ducked. Unfortunately, the ball shattered the iron bars set in the window frame, one of which cut off half the earl's face, leaving him to die in agony eight days later. More dangerous than the occasional rogue shot were the effects of massed artillery. At the siege of Murten in 1476, an observer recorded: "More than one soldier was shot apart that day, and not a few had their heads shot off."

As guns became more manageable—and more mobile—the terror which they could inflict increased in volume and accuracy. Shortly after 1400, the first effective carriages appeared, making cannons of every size more portable and more accurately aimed. By the middle of the fifteenth century, metallurgy had progressed to the point where forged barrels could be abandoned in favor of guns cast from iron and hard bronze (as opposed to the soft bronze used in bell casting). These lightweight barrels, mounted on wheeled carriages fitted with a mechanism designed to adjust the guns elevation and range, produced a weapon that could maintain repeated, accurate firing. Small guns mounted on lightweight carriages finally allowed artillery to keep up with a marching army.

Although the English first used the cannon effectively, the French proved more willing

Here we can see an early hoop-and-stave gun being brought to bear on the French by English troops during the closing decades of the Hundred Years' War. Note that one of the men-at-arms in the foreground is shouldering an early handgun.

The first hand-held weapons, like this late fourteenth-century pole gun, were crude and only effective at short range.

to adapt their castles to the needs of artillery. Whereas castles relied on high walls separated by narrow strips of open land, cannons worked best when they were placed along low walls separated by wide ditches. Castles were vertical defenses; cannons required horizontal defenses. Anxious to drive the English out of Normandy and France, the French set to work redesigning existing castles, adding bulwarks and gun emplacements beyond the outermost curtain wall and lowering existing towers to form bastions. The upper floors of towers were torn down and thrown inside the base of the tower to provide a foundation strong enough to withstand the concussion of even the biggest guns. Where traditional castles had provided a target so big that even the most awkward bombard could hardly miss them, bastions and bulwarks were too stout to be shot apart and too low to make good targets.

Although they had been unprepared for the English guns brought against them at Crécy, the French saw the cannon as a means to remain safely inside their castles and still keep the English at bay. At the second siege of Orléans in 1429, the English faced a far more astute French army. After leveling the suburbs around the walled city to provide a clear killing field for their artillery, they constructed a series of works around the castle from which they beat back the English and prevented a full-scale siege. By combining artillery in the field with improved gun emplacements in their castles, the French gradually took the initiative in the seemingly endless war. Charles VIII used his cannons to hammer away at English-held castles in Normandy

The introduction of light, portable guns revolutionized the battlefield.

Large numbers of guns could be assembled quickly, on the eve of battle, and called into action as needed.

and France with predictable effectiveness, reclaiming forty castles in one year alone, a feat that could easily have taken twenty years of fighting using conventional weapons and tactics.

After the close of the Hundred Years' War in 1453, the cannon remained at the cen-

Small and light enough for teams of four to five men to operate, the guns of the sixteenth century were a great advancement over their predecessors.

ter of King Charles's battle strategy as he fought his way across Italy to conquer the kingdom of Naples. French gunnery techniques were so feared that castles and walled cities fell before the advancing French like dominoes. The fortress of San Giovanni, which had successfully withstood a traditional siege of more than seven years' duration, capitulated in only eight hours.

As knowledge of the gun and its terrible capabilities spread, it was eagerly adopted by everyone who came in contact with it. When the Turks first captured a European gun in the late fourteenth century, the local sultan was so horrified that he ordered it dumped into the sea so that no one could ever use such a weapon again. But everyone did, including the Turks. In 1453 the Sultan Mehmet besieged Constantinople's four miles of fortified walls with sixty-nine monumentally large siege guns arrayed in fourteen batteries. The guns had a combined

Barrels cast from hard bronze and improved gunpowder provided greater range from smaller guns.

expenditure of 1,000 pounds of gunpowder per day, and some of them were supposedly large enough to hurl a stone shot weighing 1,500 pounds. These guns, combined with 258,000 men, 420 ships, and one of the most ingenious naval sieges of all time, put an end to the Byzantine Empire and Europe's dream of a Christian kingdom in Jerusalem. Buoyed by their successes in the East, the Turks attacked the island kingdom of Rhodes in 1480 so effectively that within days they had destroyed sever-

al main fortification towers and reduced the palace of the Grand Master to a heap of rubble.

By the time Columbus made his first voyage to the new world in 1492, the cannon had finally achieved the status of a fully functional element of the military and as the most decisive factor in warfare. The dominance of the armored knight and the castle on the battlefield had come to an end, but the tactics of siege warfare were to outlive them both.

The fall of Constantinople in 1453 hinged on one of the most amazing naval sieges ever executed. Access to the water passage known as the Golden Horn was essential if the Turks hoped to reach the sparsely defended sea walls on the north side of Constantinople. When the Byzantines blocked the entry to the harbor and the sea lane with a gigantic chain, the Turks were not to be deterred. While their army wore away at the land defenses on the western side of the city, Turkish engineers devised a method of bypassing the harbor chain by moving their ships over land. A wooden track was built across a narrow peninsula on the north side of the harbor. The Turkish ships were hauled out of the water, placed in wooden cradles with wheels, and towed by thousands of men across the track to the western side of the peninsula, which lay behind the defensive chain. When the astonished Byzantines realized what had happened, they were faced with nearly seventy Turkish ships in their harbor, all focusing their guns on the city. Although it required a combined assault of land and sea forces to overcome the defenses of this great city, the act of "turning the land into the sea" stands as one of the most creative siege tactics in history.

checkmate

The Decline of the Castle

In their encampment, they left all they had, trunks, beds and other things—everything except their arms—and their carts, horses and pack animals, women and servants.
—Jean de Froissart, *Chronicles*, Battle of Roosebeke

So, how stands the situation back at our siege? The French have retreated to the inner ward and the great keep because the English, through successive attacks, have over-run the outer and middle wards. The English commander knows that the French are in desperate straits as their supplies of food and water are both dangerously low. By simply blockading the defenders within the inner sanctum of the castle, the English are now playing a waiting game in an attempt to starve the garrison into submission. But this is a tactic that demands the luxury of time, and time for the English has just run out.

A messenger arrives with word from the English king. A massive French relief force is moving through the valley and lies only a few days' march from the castle. If the besiegers remain, they risk being crushed between the defiant garrison and

Here, Jean de Froissart rides through a deserted siege camp. He later described the scene: "In their encampment they left all they had, trunks, beds, and other things—everything except their arms—and their carts, horses and pack animals, women, and servants." Jean de Froissart, Chronicles, Battle of Roosebeke.

the approaching army. Their orders, therefore, are to abandon the siege and rejoin their army in the hopes of meeting the main French force in open warfare. After careful deliberation, they decide to abandon their position at night, so the besieged and beleaguered garrison will be unaware of their withdrawal and will not attempt to pursue them. They will leave behind their engines, tents, and domestic conveniences so they can travel as fast as possible. Following the decisive field battle, which they feel certain awaits them, they may (if they survive) return to reclaim some of their gear and belongings, but for now, they are off to battle—no room for pots or pans.

So this is how our siege comes to an end: no victory, no glory, just withdrawal. Which begs the question: What became of siege warfare in general? It may seem a simple enough question, but on close examination, it proves a complex issue.

Many historians have associated the decline in the castle's military importance, apparent in the fourteenth century and rapidly accelerating in the fifteenth, with the introduction of gunpowder. It is true that in the closing stage of the Hundred Years' War (1446–53), the old strongholds of western France, which had withstood so many sieges in the past, fell with astonishing speed to ponderous iron bombards; however, neither the castle nor the armored knight was automatically eliminated from war by the new firepower. In fact, both continued to take part in war throughout the sixteenth century and even later.

In history, gunpowder has often been an innovation afforded an influence on the changing face of war that it does not deserve. After the first striking demonstrations of its power as a terror weapon, its limitations were soon recognized; however, it lost neither prestige nor influence. Its immediate deficiencies in attack were that it was slow and unreliable and, on more than one occasion, unpredictable. In defense, it was as likely to damage the structure of the building that housed it as the enemy in its sights.

Until the middle of the sixteenth century, field guns were overweight, underpowered, and only semimobile. Although this was a distinct disadvantage in open battle, the siege was one of the the few arenas where artillery could be effectively brought to bear. Even the stoutest castles could not long withstand the concentrated pounding that massive bombards were capable of delivering. Castles had to evolve, and quickly, if defensive warfare was to remain

Deal Castle, built in 1539 on the order of Henry VIII, retains the familiar battlements of a medieval castle, but despite the fact that it is called a castle, its low walls and wide gun platforms clearly indicate that it is actually an entirely new type of structure.

a viable option, particularly since military tacticians began to devise ways to use cannons to the greatest effect. After their early deployment as single pieces used to defend or assault a limited area of wall—in the same manner in which siege engines had always been used—cannons began to be arranged in rows or ranks. By 1500, ordinance was common enough that batteries of thirty to forty guns were not an uncommon sight at a siege. Once set in place before a city or castle, the guns would pound the walls day and night, a punishment that even the stoutest castle could only endure for a limited time.

Plans of Henry VIII's great gun forts, clustered along England's south coast, clearly show that the rise of the cannon as a major force in warfare radically altered the shape of the well-constructed fortress.

In 1530 one of the earliest castles designed specifically to be defended by cannons was constructed at Craignethan by Sir James Hamilton. Here low, thick bastion walls were designed to withstand concentrated cannon fire. In front of the bastions were wide covered ditches into which cannon loops were placed. From these artillery emplacements—well outside the walls of the castle proper—gunners would effectively command the surrounding countryside. Thirty years later a star-shaped bastion was built at Sterling Castle on the order of Mary of Guise. The star shape allowed the cannon the greatest command of the surrounding land and provided a model for forts for the next two and a half centuries.

When the new, low-walled gun forts were originally designed, their biggest drawback was the danger of being overrun in an escalade. To prevent this, long sloping ramps were extended in front of the low-walled parapets. Built primarily of tamped earth and rubble faced with stone, these ramparts were designed to absorb the shock of incoming cannon balls while holding would-be scalers at a safe distance from the parapet walls.

Mines were still used to undermine the walls of fortified towns, but against the new bastions and gun forts they were useless. And even in the case of fortified towns, it was often faster to shoot the walls down with siege guns than to spend weeks mining them.

Therefore, while gunpowder slowly and irrevocably changed the nature of warfare in the latter Middle Ages, it is clear the castle could have been altered to meet the new challenges. Castles could be adapted to accommodate cannons. Walls could be thickened and reinforced with earthen ramparts to absorb the

shock of cannonballs. Wall walks could be widened to accept carriage-mounted cannons.[40] In chapter 2, we briefly examined the evolution of castle design and defenses. Certainly with this propensity for evolution, the castle could have been adapted to accommodate the introduction of gunpowder to the military. Something else must have been at work here.

To the military obsolescence of the castle must be added domestic obsolescence. The new gun forts were astoundingly bleak places, even by the standards of people accustomed to castle life. Half buried in the ground, with only its gun emplacements projecting above the surface, these windowless, artillery-proof forts were more like a prison than a castle. Gun forts simply did not incorporate themselves into the medieval concept of lordly living. Low and squat, there was no place for the nobility to construct commodious apartments, family chapels, and luxurious great halls.

The end of the castle, as a place of both fortification and dwelling to a great lord, actually began as early as the decades preceding and following 1400. From that point onward,

Curiously, the architectural techniques used in constructing bastions were almost identical to those used to construct the first motte and bailey castle seven hundred years earlier. An immense ditch was dug around the perimeter of a circular field and the earth excavated from the ditch was used, not to construct a motte this time, but to form an embankment around the inner edge of the ditch. This heavy earth embankment would absorb the shock of incoming cannon fire. Within the protective wall of the bastion, additional tiers of gun platforms were housed in a squat, thick-walled circular fort specifically designed to withstand cannon fire. At Henry VIII's Deal Castle, mountings for 145 cannon were aligned so as to entirely sweep the harbor in front of them. With such formidable fortifications, it is hardly surprising that invading armies could not afford to leave them intact. The art of the siege was still alive and well, but it and the rest of the world had bypassed the traditional castle.

By the fifteenth century, fewer and fewer real castles were being built. Both Bolton Castle (above) and Bodiam Castle (left), were built during the closing decade of the fourteenth century with profits taken during the Hundred Years' War. Although they both look like typical medieval castles, neither has the defensive capabilities necessary to withstand a concerted attack.

new castles tended to be castles in name only. Although they may have resembled castles, their defensive capabilities were often minimal and sometimes completely illusory. Battlements, machicolations, and arrow loops were little more than decorative affectations harking back to a more romantic time. Certainly these houses were massive enough and well enough protected by stone walls that they could have easily withstood an uprising of local peasants, but against an all-out siege mounted by an

organized army, they would have crumbled like matchsticks. The power of the castle now lay largely in its ability to inspire awe, a power not to be underestimated. If people believe a castle is unassailable, it has already done half its job.

By the beginning of the sixteenth century, the desire for ever more comfortable and elegant living quarters, which had so greatly changed the castle during the course of the Middle Ages, had created among the nobility a taste for purely residential palaces. Sometimes an old castle or part of it was radically altered into a comfortable residence with light, heat, and other amenities. In other cases, ancient keeps were allowed to decay into picturesque ruins while next to them, or in front of them, elegant new residences were built.

But substantial changes resulting in the

decline of the castle arose from more than a simple desire for domestic comforts. Perhaps the primary reason for the decline of the castle was the weakening of feudalism. An essential feature of feudalism was a group of barons supporting a decentralized government in which the principal figure was the king. Barons were men of great power, but for the most part their personal ambitions were held in check by other barons (who staunchly supported the king) and by the very considerable administrative responsibilities that their position imposed upon them. As kings and their privy councils grew stronger, the power of the barons grew less. The strong kings discouraged the building of castles, from which unruly subjects might defy them. Discouragement is one thing and complete prohibition another, so castles were still built, but in far fewer numbers. They were also less grandiose than their predecessors and were manned by permanent garrisons of professional soldiers—paid by the king—who had their own needs which, once again, influenced fortress design. We do not have time or space in this book to examine in detail all the various architectural alterations that took place in castle design and fortification, so let it suffice to say that the design and use of castles was affected by an ongoing process of change and alteration in the social and political arenas as well as in military technology.

In short, the seeds of the castle's decline are as old as the castle itself. Castles were the creation not only of a particular time and place but also of specific political and economic conditions. There was never anything more inherently permanent about a castle than about any other building; they were built to serve a particular institution or way of life. When its underlying purpose was gone, the building ceased to have any social function. Individual castles were being abandoned almost since the first ones were built. A loss of a battle or a siege, a change of government, changes of political alliances, or simply the end of a family line could at any time cause a specific castle to be abandoned. Sometimes the owner simply built a bigger castle, married into a greater estate, or lost his head by opposing the king.

Economic changes that had taken place continually since the thirteenth century also took their toll on the concept of the castle. As a mercantile economy slowly but surely replaced a purely agrarian economy, the value of land declined in comparison to trade goods and the money they generated. Needless to say, trade goods and the merchants and bankers who turned them into hard cash were found in cities, not in the countryside where most castles were located. Once the aristocracy discovered the value of commercial enterprise, they found their interests lay in the cities rather than the open spaces of farmland. As the feudal system evolved into a profit-based economy, political power, along with the substantial wealth produced by trade and the taxes on trade, began to concentrate in the hands of centralized governments—which is to say, in the hands of kings. The hell-for-glory feudal barons were losing their hold on military power, and in truth, many of them had come to prefer living well to dying gloriously.

Armies bypassed the castles that guarded vast expanses of countryside and attacked and besieged major cities and ports, anxious to plunder their wealth and seize their manufacturing capabilities. By 1380, Castle Acre was already considered of no monetary nor strategic value, and a century later the great Castle Rising Castle, on the north coast of England's Norfolk County, did not have a single building remaining under roof. In the fourteenth century, there were 380 new castles erected in England; in the fifteenth century, a mere 78 were constructed.

As we have seen throughout the book,

Haddon Hall was first fortified during the reign of King John in the early thirteenth century. Over time it was enlarged and modified, and, as war became less a threat, the modifications turned it from a functional fortress into the stately Elizabethan manor house that greets today's visitor.

the changing nature of warfare influenced both the importance and physical structure of the castle, but social conditions did as much as technology to sound their death knell. As long as land, and the ownership of land, were the ultimate source of power and wealth, the castle and its manorial estates were the most practical means of administering and protecting that wealth. As trade developed and commerce expanded, the nobility abandoned their isolated castles and moved into towns and cities in order to remain at the center of power. The empty castles they left behind were used as temporary barracks for mustering troops in time of war, or storage barns for farmers living on manorial estates. Although agricultural products were still grown on the great estates, they were bought and sold in market fairs held in cities and towns. As the source of money moved away from isolated castles, so did the seats of power, because in the Middle Ages, just as today, power always follows money.

Since the Norman invasion of England in 1066, roughly 1,700 castles have been built in England. Of these, about 700 still have visible masonry remains, but only half of this number have any recorded history. We do know that by the opening of the Hundred Years' War in 1337 nearly 20 percent of England's castles already lay in ruins. According to an inventory of castles commissioned by Henry VIII, 65 percent of Englands castles were either abandoned or lay in total ruin by 1535.

By 1500 even the massive and impregnable Caerphilly (which appears as the background for the action shots in this book) had been abandoned with the exception of one tower which was maintained as a prison. During Leylands inventory of the 1540s, Richmond castle, which had caused King John so much grief in 1215, was listed as a "mere ruin." All across England and much of Europe, castles were abandoned by the hundreds because they were of no strategic value and were too expensive to maintain simply out of tradition or a sense of nostalgia.

One of the biggest problems with the castle as an institution had always been that the building itself never produced any revenue toward its own support. Many tax rolls of the late Middle Ages note particular castles as being "valet nihil" or of no value. This is not to suggest that they played no social nor defensive value, but only that the buildings generated no income. Because castles, by their nature, tend to be huge, rambling structures, the revenue necessary to maintain them was immense. As the land on which the manorial system relied for income became less profitable than trade, maintenance of castles became an increasing drain on their owner's treasury.

When those lords who had taken to mercantile endeavors accumulated vast riches, they frequently bought up the holdings of less prosperous peers. More and more castles were falling into the hands of fewer and fewer men, but there is a limit to the number of estates any one family can maintain. Consequently, the more modern, commodious, and adaptable castles were more likely to survive than their stark and antiquated cousins.

Once the power base of the nobility was irrevocably relocated to urban centers, castles became a serious economic liability. When city councils levied for the construction of town walls, the nobility were more than happy to sell off their castles as a source of ready-cut stone to be used in the construction, often as cheap as one or two pennies per cart load.

The castle's dual life as fort and home came to an end. Military fortifications became little more than ugly bunkers with walls twenty or thirty feet thick, set deep in the ground. Noble residences were large, open "great houses" with vast expanses of glass windows—beautiful to look at, wonderful to live in, and totally indefensible.

Meanwhile, as the international economy was undergoing fundamental change, so was the nature of warfare. As we have discussed, armies of conscripted peasants were being replaced by professional armies of mercenaries and highly skilled engineers and artillerymen. With more disposable cash on hand, kings began to hire mercenaries to fill the ranks of their armies. With no castles or titles to protect, and no political goals beyond the next pay check, these professional soldiers were far easier to control than the chivalry had ever been.

In England the construction of siege castles, bastions, and gun forts was limited to the coastal areas to protect the kingdom from invasion. In the relatively peaceful interior of the island kingdom, there was little reason to build gun forts. Even during the bloody War of the Roses (1455–1485), the siege was a rarity. The armies of the Yorkists and Lancastrians—rival claimants to the British crown—slaughtered each other in the open field, avoiding both towns and cities. In reference to the fact that the English preferred field battles to sieges, Phillipe de Commynes wrote: "The realm of England enjoys one favour above all other realms, that neither countryside nor the people are destroyed, nor are the buildings burnt or demolished. Misfortune falls on soldiers and on nobles in particular." Neither side in this dynastic tug-of-war was anxious to destroy the centers of trade and manufacturing, which would bring desperately needed currency into the treasury of the winning side.

Because the expense of keeping a full-time army on the field of battle was so high, swift, decisive battles became imperative, and the siege became a luxury that was simply too costly to mount. With castles and knights having lost their military importance and sieges becoming too costly to mount, castles had become more bother than they were worth. The vast majority of the once proud castles had already been abandoned by the time the cannon actually became a decisive force on the battlefields of Europe. Once too important for

many of the castles that remained in the hands of the nobility were hastily repaired and called back into service in defense of the nobility for one last time. Those castles that were besieged and captured by parliament over the course of the war were almost universally bombarded beyond use so they could never again be defended, leaving them in the condition in which we find most of them today. Many of the castles in continental Europe remained as the seats of municipal power as late as the eighteenth century,

As the feudal system broke down, more and more fighting was done by professional soldiers, mercenaries with the skills to man increasingly complex weaponry and who could be hired and discharged as necessary. Photos courtesy of Middlealdercentret, Denmark

an army to ignore, castles were now too insignificant to attack.

Under the Swedish King Gustavus Adolphus (reigning from 1611–1632), artillery and warfare took on a recognizably modern face. Lightning strikes were backed up by lightweight guns mounted on highly mobile carriages. Before Gustavus revamped the Swedish military, it had required 1,000 horses and 220 wagons to move 36 cannons and their equipment. Five years later, 80 field pieces required the same number of horses and only half as many support wagons.

The last gasp of the medieval military monoliths can be seen in the English Civil War. During the struggle between England's King Charles I and his parliament (1642–1648),

but like their English cousins, their days of troubled glory were nearly over.

Although the castle had ceased to serve any recognizable military function, the siege would go on. By the opening of the seventeenth century, guns and forts were so well matched that sieges produced little more than protracted stalemates. The siege of Ostend, fought between the Dutch and Spanish (during the

By the seventeenth century, the castle was completely outclassed by the cannon. Like many of England's royalist castles, Corfe Castle, shown here, was reduced nearly to rubble by Parliamentarian cannons during the English Civil Wars of 1642–1649.

War of the Spanish Succession), cost nearly 70,000 lives and lasted three years.

Although castles play no active part in modern warfare, the siege is still very much alive. When the Nazi's pounded the Russian city of Stalingrad with heavy artillery in 1942, the battle fit virtually every definition of a full-scale siege. In fact, it resulted in the greatest number of people being killed as a direct result of a single battle in history. By the end of the siege, more than one million soldiers and civilians lay dead.

The theory and tactics of siege warfare can even be seen in the battle for "Fortress Britain" during World War II. The German navy and air force organized the siege using tactics dating back to the Trojan War—cut off the supplies to Britain and starve the people into surrender. German submarines attacked ships bringing in food and supplies, while aircraft battered towns and cities in the same way catapults launched boulders against castles in the Middle Ages. Like a moat, the water surrounding the British Isles prevented the Germans from launching a land-based assault. Food was carefully doled out through rationing and the people on the island fortress struggled and went hungry while their beleaguered armies sallied forth to carry the war to the enemy. Britain survived—just.

Although we no longer look to castles to impose order on a chaotic world, we find that their legacy survives all around us. It is a legacy of ambition and power, of personal property and security. It is a legacy of might makes right and he who has the biggest gun wins. It is a legacy which proves that technological advancements amount for more than skill at arms. The hundreds of castles that have survived from the Middle Ages to our own times were constructed to keep the common people and their demands on the rich and powerful under control. Today, these same castles are owned by governments that represent the people, and as a result, the castles that once withstood the poundings of brutal siege warfare have been conquered by besieging crowds of tourists that come every year to stare in awe and amazement at the greatest physical legacy of the Middle Ages.

And what more fitting end to the castle? Although they no longer prove central to the political or military security of western Europe, castles are a vivid reminder of our civilization's infancy. Their once proud walls whisper stories of great deeds and bitter political conflicts, of acts of valor and deeds of betrayal. Castles are

CHECKMATE

If you still believe that the siege was an activity particular and unique to medieval warfare, see if the following sounds familiar. On 8 September 1941, Nazi and Finnish troops headed toward the city of Leningrad from the north, south, and west. Along with the 200,000 Russian troops, the entire able-bodied population of two million set to work constructing anti-tank defenses around the city while the children, elderly, and sick were evacuated. By the first day of November, the city was completely cut off from any outside contact by air, rail, river, or road. While Nazi and Finnish troops mercilessly bombarded the city with heavy artillery, the blockade itself served as the main weapon. No accurate death counts are available, but during 1942 alone, over 650,000 Russians died—mostly from starvation, exposure, and disease, as well as from the constant shelling. The blockade and bombardment continued for 900 days, until in January of 1944, when a major Russian offensive raised the siege and drove the Germans away from Leningrad with a total combined loss of life falling somewhere between one and 1.25 million.

icons of nobility, of all that is best and worst in men; they are the physical reminder of a time when mankind dragged its way out of the Dark Ages to reinvent itself in blood and stone. Much has changed in the last six hundred years, but Europe's castles remain. Like old soldiers telling war stories to their grandchildren, castles remind us of how far we have come and yet how little we have changed.

Once a looming presence on the medieval landscape, bristling with arms and warlike men, the castle is now little more than a romantic reminder of Europe's turbulent past.

End Notes

[1] It is important to note that ancient chroniclers and creators of legend were not overly concerned with accuracy when it came to reporting events. With that in mind, we should interpret 900 towers as simply meaning that there was an impressive number of towers.

[2] It is difficult to determine exactly what form these engines may have taken, but for an in-depth examination of heavy artillery engines, see chapter 7 of this book.

[3] It should be noted, however, that there is some debate surrounding whether these dintinctive military features are indeed contemporary with the Roman Empire.

[4] The exploits of Roland and of Charlemagne's invasion of Spain are recounted in the *Chanson de Roland*, written by an anonymous jongleur as propaganda for the Crusades.

[5] It should be noted that this account was only asserted by Abbo, and his description of the machines is open to many interpretations.

[6] The earliest known example of a square keep can be found at Doué-la Fontaine in France, dated from c. 900. The surviving keep is almost entirely of 11th century construction.

[7] The trebuchet was probably a Chinese invention, adopted by the Arabs and first seen by Europeans during the Crusades.

[8] It is interesting to note that the walls of Caernarvon Castle are striped in exactly the same manner as the walls of the city of Jerusalem. Any Crusader would have recognized the patterning and sophistication of style.

[9] For a detailed discussion of gunpowder and its effect on medieval warfare, see chapter 11.

[10] *The Booke of Armes and of Chyvalrye* was written by Christine de Pisan for the king of France and would not be translated into English until Caxton printed it following the Hundred Years' War. It was unusual for a woman to write of matters military, but the worth of the text speaks for itself.

[11] It should be noted, however, that owing to the raid and retreat tactic employed by the Black Prince on this invasion, the bulk of his force was comprised of cavalry (see the Battle of Poitiers in chapter 3) which tends to travel much faster than foot soldiers.

[12] In contrast to the speed of the armies, official and commercial courier services—using relays of riders and horses—were common in the fifteenth century and could achieve remarkable speeds. In 1406 a diplomat traveled from London to Milan—a distance of 600 miles—across the Channel and the Alps, in six days.

[13] A "pipe" was a wine cask that was often used as a general unit of measure amounting to 105 gallons.

[14] One example of this may be the legendary Joan of Arc, whose very presence at the siege of Orléans was enough to convince the enemy to surrender.

[15] Early bows were made of wood, or a combination of wood and bone or horn. Later bows were made of one or more steel leaves.

[16] It is amusing to note that among those who made arrows for Lord Howard's household was one "Robard Hoode," from whom eight "shafftys" were bought on 26 September 1465.

[17] An archer always shoots or looses his bow. The only time it is "fired" is when someone puts a match to it.

[18] By the mid-fifteenth century, many continental armies (as well as the English) were employing handgunners in battle. This was a result of the shift from cavalry toward artillery previously discussed. Early gunpowder artillery in the form of cannon was also used at the siege, but its effectiveness was, at this stage, somewhat limited. A detailed discussion of gunpowder (both for hand gunners and cannon) and its effect on siege warfare may be found in chapter 11 of this book.

[19] The modern word "engineer" is intimately related to siege engines. In Latin and European vernaculars, a common term for heavy artillery devices such as the mangonel and the trebuchet was "engine" (from Latin "ingenium," meaning an ingenious contrivance). Those who designed, made, and used these machines were called "ingeniators."

[20] Roman military manuals suggest using human hair for the torsion coils of mangonel and ballista alike. Presumably, its greater elasticity and high tensile strength was preferable for the small anti-personnel engines they employed. We have been unable to find any reference to the use of hair for medieval torsion coils. Perhaps it proved less effective on larger engines, or perhaps it has to do with most of the engines' being constructed on site.

[21] The first long-range artillery weapon may have been developed in China as early as the fifth to the third century B.C. By the sixth century A.D., similar devices were in common use by both the Arabs and the Moors.

[22] The most important surviving technical work on the design, construction, and use of the perrier and trebuchet was written in 1462 by the Arab scholar Yusuf ibm Urubugha al Zaradkash and had the decorative title of *An Elegant Book on Trebuchets*.

[23] The far-reaching effects of at least one grisly trebuchet bombardment were discovered at the siege of Kaffa in 1345. While the Mongols were besieging Kaffa, their army was struck by a strange new disease. To spread the sickness among the Genoese defenders, they trebucheted the bodies of their dead soldiers into the Italian-held fortress. The escaping Genoese carried the disease home with them, and within the year, the Black Death was well on its way to ravaging the entire population of Europe.

[24] At the Siege of Acre, the bore was an axle pulled from a giant millstone.

[25] Historical illustrations of the early nineteenth century

portray the bore (inaccurately we believe) as a large screw, supposing that it would literally bore a hole in the masonry. This seems most unlikely.

[26] Charging a fortified wall (whether or not it is well defended) with nothing more than a reinforced, pointed shed would have probably proved ineffective. It is the authors' opinion that these later medieval representations are cases where the illustrators were ignorant of the tactic that they were attempting to portray.

[27] Needless to say, the idea that defenders would waste large quantities of extremely expensive oil by boiling it and pouring it down on besiegers is a myth. They used boiling water and heated sand; both had the ability to penetrate the tiniest gaps in armor.

[28] In response to the vulnerability of corners, castles progressed rapidly to designs that utilized circular towers and walls. For more information on this important design change, see chapter 2 on the evolution of castle designs.

[29] Othello, believing his wife to have been unfaithful, wished that she had been with even the lowest of the low, if only he were ignorant of the fact. He says: "I had been happy, if the general camp, Pioneers and all, had tasted her sweet body, So had I nothing known."

[30] The word "belfry" has come to be associated only with the bell tower of a church, but originally the word was "berfrei" meaning a shelter or place of refuge, which was exactly what a siege tower was intended to be.

[31] However, the next day some determined soldiers from the belfry managed to obtain a foothold upon the walls and those following swarmed into the city and opened one of the gates to let in the main army. Jerusalem was taken and the crusaders exacted a terrible vengeance on the Turks for putting up such a fierce resistance, slaughtering some 40,000 of the city's inhabitants.

[32] A cubit is an ancient measure of length, generally thought to be 18 to 22 inches. If this unit of conversion is correct, then 40 cubits equals approximately 72 feet, 50 cubits equals about 90 feet, and 60 cubits equals approximately 108 feet.

[33] A siege tower was made even as late as 1645 by the royalists during the English Civil War.

[34] In this case, a hurdle is a portable rectangular frame strengthened with withes or wooden bars, used for the erection of a temporary fence or barricade.

[35] Naturally, it would prove rather difficult to enforce such commandments, but the fact that they were issued speaks to the commonplace occurrence of these pastimes.

[36] Presumably circumventing the restriction of sumptuary laws and the prohibition against wearing men's clothing.

[37] The word "dysentery" would not be known to Froissart. This is more literally translated as "the belly-flux."

[38] It must be remembered that the term "mangonel" is widely thought to be the source of the word "gun" and that engineers who were responsible for the operation of large artillery engines were referred to as "gynours," which some historians believe to be the source of the word "gunner." Whatever the case, early chroniclers often used the terms indiscriminately.

[39] The first recorded death resulting from a handgun wound is at the battle of Agincourt in 1415. Henry V had a single handgunner among his ranks of longbowmen, and the gunner managed to get off a single shot before his weapon self-destructed. That one shot, however, found its mark and claimed what would prove to be the first of millions of future deaths by handgun.

[40] In 1945 GIs of the U.S. Forty-Second Division, for example, found the walls of Wurzburg Castle in Germany satisfactory protection against German 88-millimeter projectiles fired from across the Main River. Modern thin-shelled high explosives proved much less damaging to masonry than the stone cannonballs of fifteenth-century bombards.

Bibliography

Bartlett, C., and G. Embleton. *English Longbowmen*. London: Osprey, 1995.

Bradbury, Jim. *The Medieval Siege*. Woodbridge, Suffolk: Boydell, 1992.

Brereton, Geoffrey, tr. and ed. *Froissart's Chronicles*. London: Penguin, 1978.

Burke, John. *The Castle in Medieval England*. New York: Dorset, 1978.

Caesar: *de Bello Civili*, Book II, 8, 9.

Cantor, Norman. *Civilization of the Middle Ages*. New York: HarperCollins, 1993.

Chandler, David. *The Art of Warfare on Land*. London: Hamlyn, 1974.

Chanson de la Croisade Albigeoise. E. Martin-Chabot, ed. CHF, 3 vols., Paris, 1931–61. (Books 1–12 are by William of Tudela; the rest is anonymous.)

Chevedden P., L. Eigenbrod, V. Foley, and W. Soedel. "The Trebuchet." *Scientific American*, Vol. 273 No.1 (July 1995)

Clare, John D. *Knights in Armor*. San Diego: Gulliver, 1992.

Davis, Wm. S. *Life on a Medieval Barony*. New York: Harper, 1922.

Duby, George. *The Chivalrous Society*. Berkeley: University of California Press, 1980.

Duby, G. (ed.), and A. Goldhammer. *A History of Private Life*. Translated by Cambridge: Harvard University Press, 1988.

Duffy, Christopher. *Siege Warfare*. London: Routledge, 1996.

Dyer, C. *Standards of Living in the Later Middle Ages*. Cambridge: Cambridge University Press, 1994.

Embleton, G., and J. Howe. *The Medieval Soldier*. London: Windrow & Green, 1994.

Evans, Joan. *Life in Medieval France*. New York: Phaidon, 1969.

Fines, John. *Who's Who in the Middle Ages*. New York: Barnes & Noble, 1995.

Gies, Frances, and Joseph Gies. *Women in the Middle Ages*. New York: HarperPerennial, 1978.

——. *Life in a Medieval Castle*. New York: Harper & Row, 1979.

——. *Life in a Medieval City*. New York: HarperPerennial, 1981.

——. *Cathedral, Forge and Waterwheel*. New York: HarperCollins, 1994.

Gravett, Christopher. *Knight*. London: Dorling Kindersley, 1993.

Gravett, C., R. Hook, and C. Hook. *Medieval Siege Warfare*. London: Osprey, 1990.

Grun, Bernard. *The Time Tables of History*. New York: Simon & Schuster, 1991.

Hallam, Elizabeth, ed.. *Chronicles of the Age of Chivalry*. London: Guild Publishing, 1989.

Hassall, W. O. *How They Lived*. Oxford: Basil, Blackwell & Mott, 1962.

Higham, R., and P. Barker. *Timber Castles*. Mechanicsburg, PA: Stackpole/ Batsford, 1995.

Hill, R. *Gesta Francorum et Aliorum Hierosolimitanorum*. Oxford: Oxford University Press, 1972.

Holme, Bryan. *Medieval Pageant*. London: Thames & Hudson, 1987.

Holt R., and G. Rosser. *The Medieval Town*. London: Longman, 1990.

Hopkins, Andrea. *Knights*. London: Collins & Brown, 1990.

Houston, Mary G. *Medieval Costume in England and France*. Toronto: Dover, 1996.

Hudson, M. E., and M. Clark. *Crown of a Thousand Years*. New York: Crown, 1978.

Hunt, Tony. *The Medieval Surgery*. Woodbridge: Boydell, 1994.

James, P., and N. Thorpe. *Ancient Inventions*. London: O'Mara, 1995.

Kaeuper, R., and E. Kennedy. *The Book of Chivalry of Geoffroi de Charny*. Philadelphia: University of Pennsylvania, 1996.

Keegan, John. *A History of Warfare*. London: Hutchinson, 1993.

Kenyon, John R. *Medieval Fortifications*. London: Leichester University Press, 1996.

Koch, H. W. *Medieval Warfare*. London: Book Club Assoc., 1979.

Manchester, Wm. *A World Lit Only by Fire*. Boston: Little, Brown & Co., 1993.

Matarasso, Francois. *The English Castle*. London: Cassell, 1993.

Matthew, Donald. *Atlas of Medieval Europe*. New York: Facts on File, 1992.

McEvedy, Colin. *The Penguin Atlas of Medieval History*. London: Penguin, 1961.

McNeill, Tom. *Castles*. London: Batsford/English Heritage, 1996.

Moore, Carey. *Judith*. New York: Doubleday, 1985.

Mundy, John, and P. Riesenberg. *The Medieval Town*. Princeton: Anvil, 1958.

Newark, Timothy. *Medieval Warfare*. London: Bloomsbury, 1979.

——. *Warlords*. London: Arms & Armour/ Cassell, 1996.

Nicolle, David. *Medieval Warfare Source Book*. London: Arms & Armour/Cassell, 1996.

North, Tony, ed. *Historical Guide to Arms and Armour*. London: Studio Editions, 1994.

BIBLIOGRAPHY

Oman, W. C. *Castles*. New York: Beekman House, 1978.

Payne-Gallwey, Sir Ralph. *The Crossbow*. London: Holland, 1995.

Potter, K.R., and R.H.C. Davis. *Gesta Stephani*. Oxford: Oxford University Press, 1976.

Power, Eileen. *Medieval People*. New York: Barnes & Noble, 1969.

Reeves, Compton. *Pleasures and Pastimes in Medieval England*. Phoenix Mill, England: Sutton, 1995.

Renn, Derek F. *Caerphilly Castle*. Cardiff: Cadw, 1989.

Rothero, Christopher. *Medieval Military Dress*. Poole, Dorset: Blandford, 1983.

Sayers, D. L., tr. *The Song of Roland*. New York: Penguin, 1957.

Scott, A. F. *The Plantagenet Age: Everyone a Witness*. New York: Crowell, 1976.

Seward, Desmond. *The Hundred Years' War: The English in France 1337–1453*. London: BCA, 1996.

Singman, J., and W. McLean. *Daily Life in Chaucer's England*. London: Greenwood, 1995.

Smith, C. S., and M.T. Gnudi, tr. *The Pirotechnica of Vannoccio Biringuccio*. New York: Dover, 1987.

Soedel W., and V. Foley. "Ancient Catapults." *Scientific American*, (March 1979).

Spaulding, O. L., and H. Nickerson. *Ancient and Medieval Warfare*. New York: Barnes & Noble, 1993.

Thompson, M. W. *The Decline of the Castle*. Cambridge, England: Harvey/Magna, 1994.

Toy, Sidney. *Castles, Their Construction and History*. New York: Dover, 1985.

Vaugn, Richard, tr. and ed. *Chronicles of Matthew Paris*. Cambridge, England: Alan Sutton, 1993.

Ward, J, tr. and ed. *Women of the English Nobility and Gentry*. Manchester: Manchester University Press, 1995.

Warner, Philip. *The Medieval Castle*. New York: Barnes & Noble, 1993.

Wise, T., and G. Embleton. *Medieval European Armies*. London: Osprey, 1996.

Index